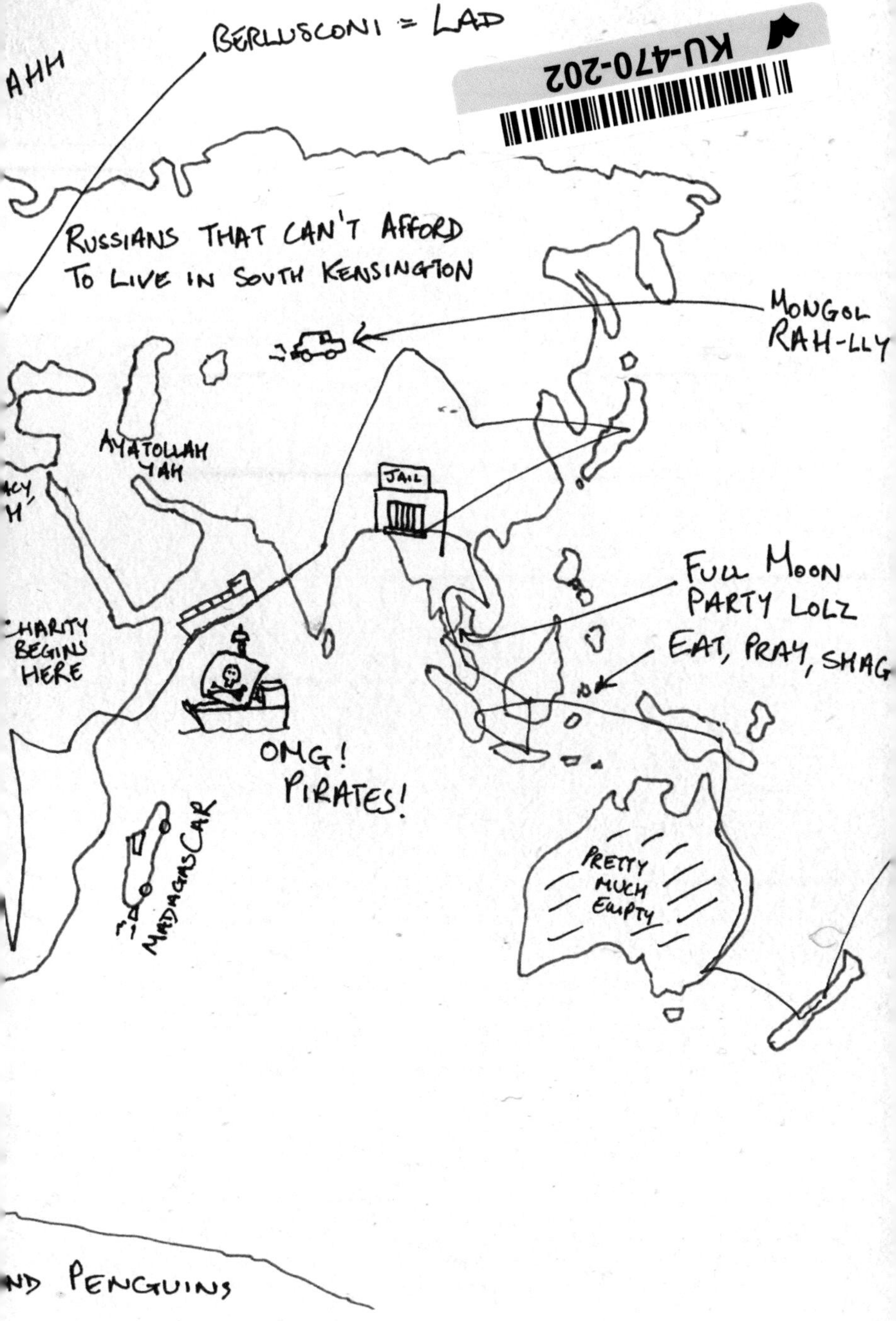
AHH
BERLUSCONI = LAD
RUSSIANS THAT CAN'T AFFORD TO LIVE IN SOUTH KENSINGTON
MONGOL RAH-LLY
AYATOLLAH YAH
JAIL
FULL MOON PARTY LOLZ
EAT, PRAY, SHAG
CHARITY BEGINS HERE
OMG! PIRATES!
MADAGASCAR
PRETTY MUCH EMPTY
ND PENGUINS

The Gap Yah Plannah

By Orlando

First published in Great Britain in 2011 by
Fourth Estate
An imprint of HarperCollins*Publishers*
77–85 Fulham Palace Road
London W6 8JB
www.4thestate.co.uk

→FULHAM, YAH

1

A catalogue record for this book is available from the British Library

BUT YOU SHOULD PROBS NOT BE SO CHEAP AND BUY YOUR OWN COPY...

ISBN 978-0-00-743206-6

Designed and typeset by Concrete Armchair
Printed and bound in Hong Kong by Printing Express

THIS PAGE IS USEFUL IF YOU'VE RUN OUT OF THINGS TO ROLL WITH

To Mummy and Daddy,
who paid for all this...

Pre-face

So, you didn't get the grades, and you've decided to take a gap yah. Or, you massively love life and want to have a cheeky beer in loads of waard places around the world, and have decided to take a gap yah. Well, you've picked up the right book. OMG, that reminds me of this time on my gap yah when I was reading a guidebook, drinking yak milk (I was in Nepal). I realised that making *my own* guidebook was the perfect opportunity to impart my wisdom about the idiosyncrasies of every country I went to, along with witty asides and amusing illustrations ... and then I JUST CHUNDERED *EVERYWAH*. Yah, all over Tarquin's *Lonely Planet*. I just shut the book and put it in the side pocket of my bag. Three months later it had dissolved, from the acid and shit. I was like, 'Have that, laminated cover! One nil!' I've stuck the little book chunklets that survived into this guide so that you can learn something. Waaardly, I didn't even need glue.

When I was Indyah, I had the literally inspired idea that I could outsource the typing of my diaries to some people thah, so I just sent them the MP3 files of me talking that I had recorded on my iPhone 4G. This was all typed by some little guy in Mumbai, but the content is pure Orlando, distilled to perfection; like the sort of home brew that will either end in a legendary night out or make you go blind. It's an epic win/fail situlashion.

After reading this, you should know the best cocktails to have in South Americah, how to do traditional African dancing, and which frogs can or cannot be licked in South-east Asiah. Or you may find out none of the above. I get distracted easily. OMG, I just saw a marmot.

Yah, so, enjoy my gap yah plannah. I made it lovingly over the course of my travels out of stuff I found, drew, printed or cut out of real books. Some other shit just ended up in here because it got stuck to the book. The legal department have asked me to 'impress upon you' that 'it's important to entirely disregard all advice given in this guide. It is meant to entertain rather than inform'. And you're not all certified L.A.D. positive like me, so probably couldn't handle the crazy shit I pull. Literally.

The noble marmot

Planning Your Gap Yah:

Where should I go?

Three words for you: ***cash-lash ratio***. So important that I've underlined it. You're probably thinking, 'Oh, this is easy – the more povo countries will have cheaper beer.' I would say: first of all, you shouldn't use the word 'povo' (it's 'less economically developed'); and secondly, shut up.com, you're wrong. Many things affect the golden ratio, other than how cheap everything else is in a country. The first is a drinking cultyah. As anyone who has been to France will tell you, a pint costs, like, ten pounds. They sit there sipping, and talking about films and philosophy and shit rather than getting massively lashed, and as a result their beer costs loads more than in Britain as they don't shift as much booze every night. Other places that might be cheap for other stuff are also expensive for beer because everyone's a Muslim and so booze is illegal. This is what Malaysiah is like, and you have to get a dealer to smuggle the beers in. While making lashing feel more illicit and therefore more fun, you do lose a lot of value. Anyway, to help you out, I've drawn a helpful cash-lash map below.

- Expensive
- OK
- Green light to LASH!

What should I do?

Charidee. It's the gap yah gift that keeps on giving. Usually, if you say to someone, 'Will you pay for me to go on holiday for a whole year?', they say, 'NO. How did you get into my office? Who are you?' But replay the same scenario when you're doing charidee – and they give you money. It's tax-deductible for the people who give you money (and if there's one thing rich people like, it's not paying tax), the orphans get a school/hospital/llama sanctuary, and you get an excuse to get on the lash train to a foreign country. And you can then tell everyone about what you spent your year doing in order to raise better awahhness. Anyway, just find a charity project in a country with a good cash-lash ratio, and you're literally sorted.

When should I take my gap year?

Take one straight after school, then another just after university, then another when you feel like it because work is lame.

Who should I go with?

Introducti

This is from my travel blog which I write for a paper called the *Guardian*:

Orlando Charmon

Unfortunately, you also meet loads of really boring people who keep wanting to talk about museums and shit

A lot of people say that to get the real spiritual, political and cultural experience of travelling, you should do it on your own, and it is quite fun travelling on your own, as you're more likely to banter some serious characters. Unfortunately, you also meet loads of really boring people who keep wanting to talk about museums and shit, and you end up travelling with them because you alienated most of the rest of the hostel by taking a shitload of special-K and spending the evening rubbing your face against the wall of the communal dormitory and snarling. So, the best thing to do is to have both experiences. Initially, go travelling with a big group of friends and arrange to do the charity projects together (this is especially important, because someone from your group of friends will have a dad who's mega-rich and will probably just pay for the whole thing). Then after a few months, you will inevitably have a massive falling out – especially if this is a mixed-sex group – and you can all spend a few days breaking up into factions and cliques before storming off and saying that no one else really 'gets' the experience. You're then free to go off travelling on your own or with the boring Swedish archaeology enthusiast, who is the only person you haven't managed to massively piss off.

> 'you can all spend a few days breaking up into factions and cliques before storming off and saying that no one else really 'gets' the experience'

Right; Boring Swedish Archaeology students generally look like this.

I'd just left my notebook lying around the other day, when a guy was like, 'I hope you don't mind, I just glanced at your diary over your shoulder. I see you're going on a gap year?'

I'm just like, 'Literally no worries. I'm going to publish it anyway.'

And then he offered me a job writing a travel blog for this newspaper thing. So the banter above was from the first post, and it's been getting a great response – everyone has been commenting on it. I should probably mention that the guy who offered me the blog was my uncle, rather than just a random though, otherwise the story doesn't make sense.

Spinklechode
14 August 2011 11:41AM

Recommend? (10)

Report abuse

Clip| Link

This comment, and several other personal attacks on author, deleted by moderator

Recommend? (0)

Report abuse

Clip| Link

Are you Jonathon Charmon's nephew?

Blingbong
14 August 2011 12:01PM

Recommend? (8)

Report abuse

Clip| Link

I can't believe that. Why has this guy got a blog and not me??? I graduated from Goldsmiths College with a degree in journalism, and this guy is just some nineteen year-old chump! I hate you Guardian! Although my CV is available on request. I did several pieces for the Purley and Coulsdon Advertiser that caused quite a stir. I look forward to hearing from you. Best regards, David Preston

BumYoghurt
14 August 2011 12:48PM

Recommend? (10)

Report abuse

Clip| Link

I am literally sick to the back teeth of having to see/listen to all of these posh mummies' boys who have never lived a day in reality of their lives talking like they have a clue about anything. They need to come down to Glasgow, we'll drink 10 pints then I'll glass the cunts. That's living. Not this gap year shit.

benzedrain
14 August 2011 12:49PM

Recommend? (0)

Report abuse

Clip| Link

This Orlando guy sounds like a total fuckpig.

Tarquin88
14 August 2011 01:06PM

Recommend? (0)

Report abuse

Clip| Link

This is a great blog! I ROFLed so hard, it was an absolute LOLercaust

3

gimboid77
15 August 2011 02:00AM

U cant be serios!!! Dis is da worst eva.

FluffyKitten
15 August 2011 02:30AM

God, this guy is just like the Nazis. You know, the way they took Ketamin

Unknown user
15 August 2011 12:02PM

Hey gr8 blog! Check out mine – www.lemonparty.org

Surperior
15 August 2011 12:29PM

Whoever wrote this doesn't have a clue

Surperior
15 August 2011 12:30PM

Whoever wrote this doesn't have a clue

Myballsache
15 August 2011 12:49PM

I can't believe I just red this. Finding this in my usually liberal newspaper is the journalistic equivalent of coming home to find out that someone has dirty protested ur bedroom. U don't know why it's there, but it sure stinks.

What should I bring?

1. Jack Wills summer season wardrobe – this pretty much covers everything you need to wah.
2. A massive bag – make sure it's the sort that an explorer would have. It needs capacity not only for all the clothes you bring out but for all the spears, carved wooden masks and ironic statuettes of cocks that you want to buy. Also, make sure it has loads of zips – if people in your dormitory annoy you, do loads of zipping and unzipping when you come in from a night out. Nothing more annoying when you're trying to get to sleep.
3. Flip-flops with Brazilian flags on them – I don't know why, but we all have these.

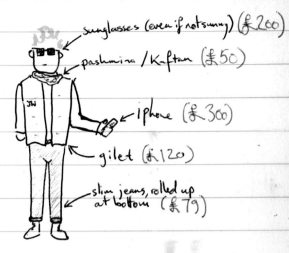

sunglasses (even if not sunny) (£200)

pashmina / Kaftan (£50)

JW

iPhone (£300)

gilet (£120)

slim jeans, rolled up at bottom (£79)

Fig 2. Dress to Impress

4. Your iPhone — so you can update Facebook with where you
    are, saying hilarious things like 'I'm in Ulaanbataar,
    Mongolia. More like UlaanBANTER!!!! ROFLMAO!!!'
5. Your Blackberry — someone might BBM you.
6. An extra old phone (iPhone 3GS) — foreign countries are
    like festivals, there's not always an opportunity to
    charge your phone, so have a spare spare phone.
7. One of those Sigg bottles — to keep your gin cold, you
    lash hero.
8. 4-season sleeping bag — make sure it's expensive enough to keep
    you warm in the North Pole, even if you only use it in hostels.
9. Money — this is useful in most situations.
10. Your passport — otherwise, when you're arrested, you'll
    be treated like the rest of them.
11. A copy of *War and Peace* — you probs won't read it, but
    you should carry it around with you anyway so that you
    can have a raally battered copy on your bookshelf when
    you start uni.
12. More money tucked into your sock — back-up bribing stash.
13. A guitar — people will then gather around to listen to
    you play. All you need to learn is 'Wonderwall'. Others
    will take over after that.
14. A soft toy — tie it to your bag as a mascot. This makes
    you look approachable and lighthearted. It'll get dirty,
    but that'll show how much travelling you've done.
15. Hand sanitiser — in case you touch one of the charity people.
16. A sense of adventyah — don't ever let anyone tell you
    that it can't be done, or that it's 'illegal'. These are
    just words they use to try to crush our spirit.

What's my budget?

What's my credit card limit?

But seriously, you'll need some money to get out on your travels and this will require some fundrahsing. Maybe do a club night or some shit like that. Though once you've got enough to get out there and cover travel, you can just emotionally blackmail your parents into picking up the tab for all your other costs. I wrote down the spending I could remember after my trip. This is at the back of the book I think.

How will I organise it?

Get someone else to organise it for you. I paid a company called STI Travel to sort out my gap yah. Generally in life, it's better to get other people to do stuff for you. Saves time.

✚ Health & Safety

INSURANCE — Get it, as you'll probably need it when you inevitably maim yourself. If you don't maim yourself, you're not trying hard enough.

DODGY TAXIS — Apparently not all taxis are licensed and stuff, so may be just scammers who intend to rob you. Guidebooks suggest that you should take a note of the registration number of any taxi you take. I suggest you do this on your iPhone — you can then email it to yourself, so you still have it after they steal your iPhone.

DOS AND DON'TS

DO:

- Read my book before you go. Otherwise you'll have no banter for all the randoms you meet.
- Contact the relevant embassy or consulate to see if they have any parties going on, and tuck in to the Ferrero Rocher.
- Have extra copies of your passport for when you lose it. It's important to have a silly photo on your actual passport to amuse border guards and the like. When the passport people reject your passport photo, you just write to them, pretending to be a doctor:

To whom it may concern,

My patient, Orlando Charmon, exhibits a facial tic due to a properly serious rare congenital disorder. This picture is an accurate representation of his face.

Yours sincerely,

Dr Ernest Chunderford

SHIT, IT's EXPIRED!?

- Make sure that friends and family are awah of your travel itinerary, so they can get raally jealous.

DON'T:

- Live your life by saying 'don't'. Man up and take a gap yah.

South America

South America
Notes:

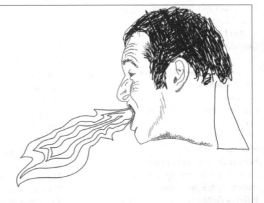

Information and maps

South America. Like North America, but almost entirely different. From the hot tropical climes of the Amazon basin to the heady heights of the Peruvian Andes, South America has a greater range of climes and climbs than your average continent. This variety extends to activities too: whether you want to go white-water rafting, mountain climbing or be kidnapped by revolutionary agrarian anti-imperialist Marxist-Leninist guerrilla soldiers, you can find it all in South America.

1

I first flew into Perah, travelling down through Chile and Argentinah before going back up through Uragay (Yes you are. Banter!), Brazil, Venezuelah and Colombiah. After that, I pretty much wasn't welcome on the continent.

Extra things to bring:

1. A money clip – a lot of South American currencies have devalued a lot. Money clips are also useful for easy access to money, in case you want to 'make it rain' in a club.

2. A snuff box – so you can feel like an eighteenth-century drug fiend, should you be partial to a bit of 'naughty salt'.

3. A man-thong/full bikini/nipple tassels – if you're going to Brazil, you need to be ready for carnival. Anything goes.

4. Your dancing shoes – these are metaphorical. Literally.

5. Rennies/gout medicine – eating red meat three times a day in Argentinah plays hell with digestion.

6. A Che Guevara T-shirt – they love him here. Although I think at one point he wasn't so popular with some Bolivians …

7. A motorcycle – Che Guevara rode a motorcycle, so should you.

8. A cigar cutter – Che Guevara smoked cigars, so should you.

9. A copy of *Das Kapital* – Che Guevara instituted agrarian reform on a socialist footing, so should you.

10. Stuff to give to, like, orphans and stuff – loads of charity work to do all over South America. You can kinda change the world in a week, and then get some serious travelling in.

11. Yellow fever, typhoid and tetanus vaccinations – or you could probs just take some homeopathic medicines? They're probs just as effective. I'm not a trained aromatherapist, but I think echinacea will probs ward off all those diseases.

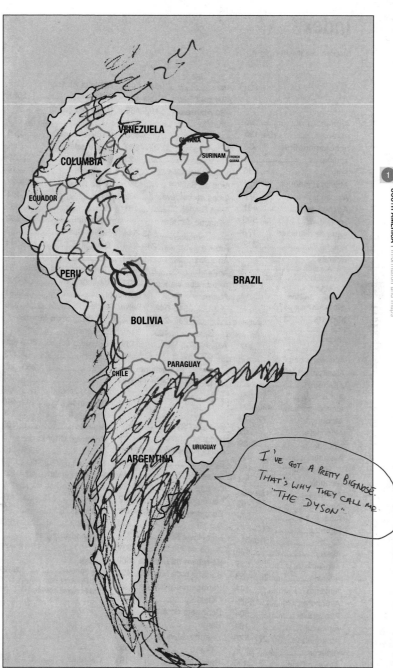

Orlando's Diary: Perah

'Japes on a plane'

So, it turns out when they tell you to get to the ahrport two
ahrs early, they're not joking, as ahrplanes do actually leave
without you if yah're not thah. Basically, there was a massive
night going on in Boujis — you know Boujis? Yah, Boujis — the
night before, and I was like, 'OMG, I can't believe how ahrly
I have to be up fah this plane!!!' I should probably just
have had one or two, but it turned out that it was Soos's
birthday (I think she's one of Venetia's friends — which was
a bit awkward.com, as I had broken up with Venetia the week
before — you don't want to have a gf on your gap yah. Obv.)
and, like, all the lads from school were thah. Tarquin was
just like, 'I can't believe we're losing your shit chat for
a whole yah!' I was like, 'STFU Tarquin. You've got shit chat.
Er, could someone open a window please? Cos Tarquin's chat is
stinking out the place.' Everyone was like, 'Ooh, massive
burn.' Then Tarquin was like, 'Whatever, let's get the drinks
in,' and Rory's like, 'Cheeky Jägerbomb?' I knew I had my
plane at a literally unholy hour the next day, so I just
said, 'Nah, you're OK — shouldn't hit it too hard.' Rory looks
at me like I was a chav: 'Did someone order a Gay? Cos one's
over thah!' Rory was rugby captain, so he had a few cronies
to laugh at his joke around him. Basically, before I knew it,
I had sunk ten Jägerbombs just to prove that I was still
'Fidel Lashtro', as the lads call me.

Next thing I know, I wake up. I've passed out at the kitchen
table. There's a carton of Waitrose not-from-concentrate orange
and mango juice in front of me, and a half-eaten artisanal
chorizo sausage. All my stuff is at the door and I've got my
plane ticket in front of me, but it's not too useful as the
departure time was two ahrs ago. My phone has, like, ten missed
calls from the parents. They're in Tarquin's parents' place in
Yorkshire for the weekend on a shooting trip. I'm so annoyed
because I SO wouldn't have missed the plane if they'd bothered
to say goodbye to their son, who's literally going to be gone
for a yah. I rang my old man.

'You've missed your plane then.'

'Well, yah, I've obv missed my plane, otherwise I
wouldn't be ringing you.'

'Business class lets you make calls. Or your plane
could be delayed.' My old man can be such a knobber sometimes.

'Could you maybe be a bit more unhelpful please?
Yah, thanks. God, I can't believe I rang you.' I was about
to hang up when my old man was like, 'I've organised you
another plane. It leaves in four ahrs from Heathrah. Think
you can make it?'

So I got the plane, but because it was booked late, I had
a six-hour stopover in George Bush international ahrport,
Texas. You would have thought that would be enough time to
pass through American customs, but literally I had to run
all the bits that I wasn't queueing for. Am I a person who:

'ordered, incited, assisted, or otherwise participated in the persecution of
any person because of race, religion, national origin, or political opinion
under the control, direct or indirect, of the Nazi Government, or of the
government of any area occupied by, or allied with, the Nazi Government
of Germany, or who participated in genocide in any country'?

WTF? How many people answer yes to that? Got into a bit of
an argument with the CIA about that one. It didn't help that
I was absolutely hammered, as it turned out they give you free
booze in business class. I thought I may as well start as I
meant to continue, but the problem with a flight that long is
you can get drunk, hit hangover, and then get drunk again,
all in the space of one flight, which is what I did, obv.
Eventually I got to Perah.

The first stop on my big round-the-world trip. Perah. First week
was spent in a Spanish language school (may as well get some CV
points while I'm here). It was a bit rubbish, but at least I
learnt all the important phrases - una cerveza por favor! - and
had a look round Lima, which is by and large pretty boring. It
looks a bit like Croydon, or at least what I imagine Croydon to
look like. I've obviously never been there. Anyway it all looked
a bit shit, but I was starting the adventyah of a lifetime!!!!!

Foreign and Commonwealth Office Advice:

- Around 67,000 British tourists visit Peru every year. Most visits are trouble free.

  `This means that you probably have to try quite hard to cause`
  `trouble. But I would say follow your dreams.`

- Due to the unprecedented current cold weather, the Peruvian government has declared a state of emergency in all districts over 3,000m above sea level and parts of the Peruvian Amazon.

  `As a disaster-hit area, they probably definitely want a`
  `Western presence to oversee rebuilding work. If you're`
  `interested in charity work, you should probably head here.`
  `Don't worry about any previous experience in reconstruction.`

- Drug trafficking is a serious crime in Peru and drug smugglers face long terms of imprisonment.

  `(You can probably pay your way out of this...)`

- Driving standards in Peru (particularly in Lima) are poor. Crashes resulting in death and injury occur frequently.

  `This means that even if you don't have a driving licence,`
  `you can probably have a go. You can't be any worse than`
  `the Peruvians.`

- You are **not** allowed to take any valuable archaeological artefacts from the country without the proper authority.

  `You can probably just pretend you bought it from a street`
  `market, or carved it yourself, though. Most of that so-called`
  `archaeological shit looks home-made anyway.`

History of Peru:

Peru's most famous citizen is, of course Paddington Bear, but so much more happened in that country before everyone's favourite marmalade enthusiast made it famous. Humans arrived in the Americas roughly 20,000 years ago, and hunted animals such as giant sloth, sabre-toothed tigers and mastodons, which are now extinct. It's a great shame that such animals have been lost to the ecosystem.

`LOL! Literally would love a sabre-tooth tiger rug. They would`
`have been epic to hunt! A bit like the time I went hunting at`
`Tarquin's house and accidentally shot his sister's pony.`

Domestication of the llama, alpaca and guinea pig had begun by about 4000 BC. As all of these could be deep-fat fried, this considerably improved quality of life.

Around the 1430s, the Incas established an empire by conquering neighbouring peoples. The Incas, whose emperor was believed to have descended from the sun (LAD), formed an elite and made everyone they conquered work for them and keep them in a lifestyle of luxury, travelling, riding llamas and sacrificing virgins.

WATCH OUT, TARQUIN!!! LoL.

Fig. 3. A llama

Unfortunately for the Incas, they were discovered by the Spaniards in the 1520s, and the Spaniards had a magpie-like lust for shiny things. The Incas only had weapons made of rocks and sticks, and armour made of gold – compared to the steel-breastplated gun-toting Spaniards on horseback – so they stood little chance when it came to pitched battles. Despite being massively outnumbered, Pizarro and his Conquistadores managed to capture the Incan emperor, which was clearly troublesome for the Incas as he was the living personification of the Sun-God.

Peru eventually gained independence from Spain in the nineteenth century and became a republic. Despite some wars with neighbours through its history and an internal Maoist uprising, it is now largely stable.

If your parents are like, 'Oh we don't want you to go to some politically unstable place and get caught up in a revolution', you can be like, 'I'm literally not. Read this history bit. Can I have fifty pounds please? I'm going out to the Sloaney Pony. What? OK, whatevs, forty then, but you're the worst parents ever. God, you're so embarrassing.'

According to the UN World Drug Report 2010, Peru displaced Colombia as the world's top producer of coca leaf, the raw material used to make cocaine. In 2009, Peru produced 119,000 tonnes of coca versus 103,100 tonnes in Colombia.

Cocaine production is like South America's version of the Premier League. Foreign owners, overpaid players and little benefit to the local economy.
A guy said that to me. Satiri-banter.

PERUVIAN

Orlando Charmon reports for *The Lady* from Lima

Culture

Peruvians are quite formal, and a bit weirded out if you kiss them the first time you meet them. They're more into the handshake. Basically treat them like your dad.

They are also not against throwing rocks at stray dogs. So try not to be too offended if this should happen in your presence. If you see a stray dog, throw a rock at it. It's pretty cultural.

ARTS AND MUSIC

Peru's most famous novelist is the Nobel Prize-winning Mario Vargas Llosa. He was probably a better novelist than a politician, as he ran for the presidency in 1990 and lost.

Not everyone can combine being a former House Captain at school, and writing a bestselling guidebook. I didn't want to be Head Boy anyway, because they only pick lame people who do everything the teachers say.

As to music, the Peruvians love panpipes. They also play a litany of instruments such as ocarinas, seashell horns, guitars made of armadillo shells and rattles made of goat hooves.

as

Basically, whatever you've got leftover after dinner, poke a few holes in it and you have a Peruvian instrument.

Techno-cumbia trance music is popular amongst the youth.

`Epic Win!!!`

FOOD & DRINK

When you come out here, you should probably start viewing the guinea pig not as a treasured childhood pet, but as a delicious deep-fried rat. Peruvians love eating guinea pig – there's even a painting of the last supper in Cuzco cathedral featuring guinea pig as the main course.

The best hangover cure is *sopa a la criolla*, a spiced noodle soup with beef, milk and peppers which is often topped with a fried egg perched on a toast raft.

`An edible floating egg ship!!!`

`Legendary.`

You should probably try *anticuchos de corazón*, shish kebabs of grilled beef hearts.

`Eat your heart out!`

`Beer! Yes! Cuzqueña is a massive win. Literally drank ten on my first day. If you're getting your lash on, you should probably also try a Malta, a dark beer, and Pisco Sour, the national cocktail. If you really want to man up, mix them all together. Just ask for an 'Orlando' anywah in Cuzco. They'll make it up for you.`

```
pre...
chunder ...
not chunklets ...
```

The Lady 57

Language: *Peru*

Un millón de cervezas por favor – A million beers, please.

Estoy borracho – I'm lashed.

Estoy en mi año de vacío – I'm on my gap yah.

Pedazo – Chunklet.

Vomcán – Vom-cano.

Vomité en su zampoña – I chundered in your panpipes.

Qué es la broma? – What's the banter?

Puede poner algún dubstep? – Can you put on some dubstep?

Eso es lo que tu mamá dijo – That's what your mum said.

```
(a useful one for an icebreaker - i.e.: 'How are you
today?' 'I'm pretty tired.' 'Eso es lo que su mamá dijo!'
After all the sex! Banter!)
```

Country no 2. **BOLIVIA:**

Wonderful. Raaaally spiritual.

Country no 3. **CHILE:**

Foreign and Commonwealth Office Advice:

- If you are a British national resident in or travelling to Chile we encourage you to register your contact details with LOCATE, the Foreign and Commonwealth Office's online consular registration service.
  - This is important. Your parents might want to post you a new credit card.

History of Chile:

The first European to reach Chile was Magellan in 1520 whilst on a journey to circumnavigate the globe. Magellan = Lad on tour!!! It is in his honour that the Strait of Magellan, on the southernmost tip of the continent, is named.

Note to self: get something named after me.

It became independent from Spain in 1818, after a period of warfare, and Bernardo O'Higgins took the role of supreme dictator.

Chilean Culture:

Lifestyle

Chilean police aren't as easily bribed as other places on the continent. They even arrest you if you try to bribe them.

Arts and Music

Chile's national dance, the *cueca*, is worth a try while you're here. It's like a sexy version of Morris dancing. You'll never see thigh-slapping and handkerchiefs in the same way again.

The oldest art in Chile is rock art. A particularly interesting example can be seen in the outline paintings of hands near Villa Cerro Castillo

It literally wasn't very good. I drew a cartoon badger next to them to show everyone how much better I could draw, so look out for that.

Kuntsman is a popular Chilean beer.
New drink of choice - just for the name!!!

Jote, which is wine mixed with coke, is also popular.
WTF??

Have you ever wanted to go to a strip club at lunchtime? The jugs in the Café con Piernas aren't just for coffee. Basically, in order to get the fledgling coffee industry off the ground, café owners decided to have half-naked staff. Beats Starbucks ...

Orlando's Diary: Chile

'Red Hot Chile Gapper'

Flew to Chile from Perah on a little plane so that I could see the Nascar lines. They reminded me a bit of the time that it snowed at school and me and the guys walked in a line to draw out a massive picture of a cock on the playing field. The Nascar drivers who made these lines were a bit more imaginative (but less funny) and did like loads of pictures of spiders and stuff.

So I'm only in Chile for, like, two days, but on the way through to Santiago I popped into Boliviah to get my passport stamped. Why not? I knew, like, someone would be like, 'Yah, so I did Boliviah last year,' and I wanted to be like, 'Oh yah, it's wonderful, isn't it? Raaaally spiritual.' Which I couldn't legitimately do if I hadn't been thah. So that filled a chapter, didn't it? Five minutes well spent.

Anyway, Chile looks nice. I went to one of the stripper cafés, but didn't stay long. Mostly because they kept shouting at me. I tried to point out that actually serving hot coffee with so little clothing on was an accident waiting to happen. Probably just going to stick to Starbucks from now on. Chile turned out to be much more expensive than expected, and the cash-lash ratio wasn't great. I decided to bin it and head to Argentinah.

Language: *Chile*

Agarrón – To feel. *(Is the act of touching private parts of the body. This may happen with or without permission.)*

Barsa – Shameless. - They kept saying this to me for some reason.

Choro – Bad Ass. - This is literally me.

Prendido – On Fire.

(Used as a way of saying someone is a party animal.) - If you're a real hero you can combine both meanings ...

Esa onda - OMG!!!

Pintar monos – Try to catch everyone's attention by being foolish. - This seemed to come up a lot.

Tener caña – Being hungover.

Country no 4. **ARGENTINA:**

Foreign and Commonwealth Office Advice:

- There is a risk of 'express kidnappings'. `Saves time in the long run though ...`
- There have been some recent protests against British interests in Argentina in the context of tensions over current hydrocarbon explorations off the Falkland Islands. You should avoid any area in which large crowds are gathering. `Unless you're wearing your Che Guevara T-shirt.`

History of Argentina:

The history of A̶̶̶̶̶̶̶̶̶̶̶̶̶̶ by historians into four main sections: the pre-Columbi̶̶̶̶̶̶̶̶̶̶̶̶ to the 16th century), the colonial period (roughly 1516 to 18̶̶̶̶̶̶̶̶̶̶̶̶ early post-colonial period of the nation (1810 to 18̶̶̶̶̶̶̶̶̶̶ around 1880.

The begin̶̶̶̶̶ ̶̶̶he first human s̶̶̶̶ writter̶̶̶ Juan̶̶̶

Sp̶̶ V̶̶

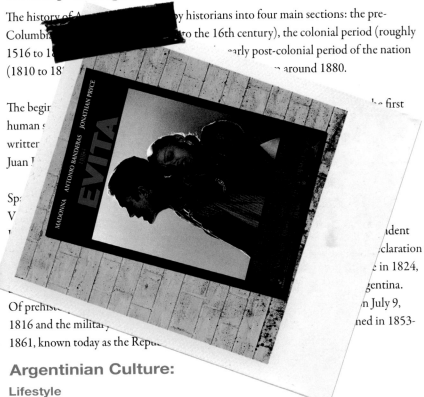

̶̶̶dent ̶̶̶claration ̶̶ in 1824, ̶̶entina.

Of prehis̶̶̶̶ ̶̶n July 9, 1816 and the militar̶̶̶ ̶̶ned in 1853-1861, known today as the Repu̶̶̶

Argentinian Culture:

Lifestyle

Argentinians like kissing a lot more than the Peruvians; even the men kiss as a greeting. If you're not used to kissing men, it can take you a bit by surprise – especially when you accidentally make lip-to-lip contact with an old man.

If you're making more lip-to-lip contact and want to take it further, Buenos Aires is furnished with a glut of 'telos', which are pay-by-the-hour sex hotels of varying degrees of sleaziness. Pick one to suit your taste (and budget ...)

Sport

The Argentines enjoy a variety of sports and have achieved successes on the internation[al] stage including two victories at the football world cup where they were aided by footba[ll] legend Diego Maradona. They also play rugby and a version of polo called *pato* (which literally translates as 'duck').

Food and Drink

As one of the world's major producers of meat, especially beef, Argentine cuisine show[s] a clear preference for meaty dishes, making Argentines the largest consumers per capit[a] of beef in the world.

After a while, you start to get the meat sweats, but once you push through that barrier, you emerge as more of a lad. Steak for breakfast, steak for lunch, steak for dinner. All washed down with gout medicine and red wine.

Language: *Argentina*

Ciertamente oficial. Repondré mis pantalones en seguida.

– Certainly officer, I'll put my trousers back on right away.

Quite por favor las esposas. Tengo dinero!

– Please take off the handcuffs. I have money!

Yo no puedo sentirme la cara. Qué estuvo en eso?

– I can't feel my face. What was in that?

Yo no puedo sentirme las pelotas. Temo que pueda haber contratado algo.

– I can't feel my balls. I fear I may have contracted something.

Yo no puedo sentirme los senos. Ah sí, por supuesto. Son tus senos. Yo no tengo senos.

– I can't feel my breasts. Ah yes, of course. They're your breasts. I don't have breasts.

Broma! – Banter!

BEFORE:

AFTER:

BROMA!!

BROMA??

DIEGO MARADONA

Orlando's Diary: Argentinah

'Don't buy for me Argentinah'

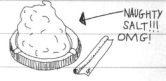

NAUGHTY SALT!!! OMG!

So, I'm staying at this hostel in the centre of BA, called
Milhouse. Not sure if it's named after the Simpsons
character. This place is crazy, if a bit touristy. They're
not raally proper travellers like me. I'm in this
dormitory, shared with a couple of Israelis, a German and a
South African. The South African (I think his name was
Schaaalk) has just come back from playing rugby. 'I tell
you, bru, thise Argies wud eat a soft nirthin himisphere
buy like you. You dun't know what rrrugby is like here.' I
talk to him for a bit, but there's a pretty massive
language barrier in that I have literally no idea what he's
saying. Across the room, thah's an argument going on
between the Israelis and the German. They're calling each
other 'expansionist' because they're both using a spare
bunk for their stuff. I watch this for a bit, and video it
on my phone — they sound quite funny arguing in English.
'ZIS iz not ARCCEPTIBLE!!!' Massively YouTube material.

Then a guy comes in. I'd been chatting to him earlier about
the dubstep scene in Argentinah. Apparently there isn't one.
He's obviously already bang on it — pupils like saucers. The
Israelis and German stop and look at him — mostly because
he's wearing flashing glasses and a T-shirt that lights up —
and he's just like, 'Hey guys, chill out. This is Argentina.'
They pretty much can't argue with that, especially when the
argument is made by a six foot six, slightly balding Spaniard
covered in flashing lights. He's rummaging in his bag when
he, like, sees me: 'Heey guy. You still gonna party
tonight??' Foreigners literally love saying 'party'… But I'm
just like, 'Yah, whah?' and he tells me about a secret club
that only the taxi drivers know about. At first, I don't
really get why he wants to go to a club full of taxi
drivers. Sounds literally boring, but very convenient. But
he's like, 'It's underground, you know, special produce. Keep
moving club, and no police. It's cool, man. You jus gotta
ask taxi for Route 66.' I'm just like, 'Yah, let's get this
banterwagon cruising down Route 66!' He obviously has no idea
what I'm talking about, but repeats it because he knows
whatever I've said is pretty cool.

The taxi pulls up, and Javez pays the guy — he got it much
cheaper than usual, probs cos he's, like, able to speak the
lingo. All the same, I'm not too convinced by whah we've

been dropped off. It's like a random house in a suburb. We go up and knock on the door. After a while, a little thing in the door slides across and a guy looks out through it. A few bolts slide back and a massive guy opens the door, looking around the whole time. Often, the nastier the bouncers look, the better the club turns out to be.

Inside, there's more powder than I've ever even seen skiing in Val d'Isah. Literally, this place was a blizzard. I go up to the bar and order the same thing as Javez does and we sit down. Turns out that a gram comes with a free beer. Bargain! Opposite us is a guy who looks exactly like Maradona. He's got a girl either side of him and an ashtray full of coke. He's living the dream.

Anyway, things turn a bit hazy after this. I was already pretty well on my way to Lashville, Tennessee by the time we reached Route 66, so that's probably not surprising. Next thing I know, I'm sitting on a bench next to Javez. Well, I suppose it would be more accurate to call it a pew, because we're in, like, a church. There are loads of statues around and, like, old people mumbling about Jesus. Javez is joining in with the praying shit, clearly miles away mentally, and still wearing his flashing glasses. I look up at the front, and who is it giving the mass, literally dressed up in a priest robe and stuff? Maradona lookalike from last night. At this point I'm not sure whether I'm hallucinating, so I turn to go, and there's a girl next to me. I vaguely recognise her from the night before. She's just like, 'You wanna go?' And I decide to get the hell outta thah with this random girl. Basically autopilot must have taken over at this point, because we decide to have a beer and one thing leads to another, which leads to a telo.

Next morning I wake up, and there are two middle-aged women shouting at me. I'm massively confused but they point to my wallet, which is literally empty of money. I'm also pretty sure there was an iPod thah too, and that's missing. The random girl is gone. It takes a while, but I realise the middle-aged women are chambermaids, and they must have clocked that the girl robbed me, but I can't be bothered in the end to report it. I just stride out into Buenos Aires to get some breakfast. It turns out that she left my credit cards and my phone, so I must have been pretty good in the sack. I'm happy to write off the money and iPod as banter tax for such a massive night out.

Country no 5. **BRAZIL:**

I remember very little of Rio. Apparently, if you can remember carnival, you weren't thah. Some things are probably best to forget. Still, as they say, what goes on tour, goes on Facebook! ;)

rlando 👍 Like

Wall   Info   Photos   YouTube   Discussions

rlando has uploaded 62 photos in the album 'Carnivom!!!'

Top 5 things to do in Rio de Janeiro

1. Stroll through the botanical gardens

2. Explore the Bohemian neighbourhood of Santa Teresa

3. Shop for souvenirs at the artisan market

4. Take in the views from Corcovado and Pão de Açúcar

5. Hike through Tijuca National Park.

Literally did none of these. Too busy having an epic time at carnival!!!!!

HOW TO DRESS AT CARNIVAL. AN ILLUSTRATED GUIDE:

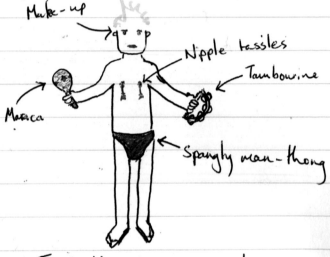

Make-up

Nipple tassles

Tambourine

Maraca

Spangly man-thong

Fig 3. How to carnival

Language: *Brazil*

O meu bocal tassles parecem ter se tornado enredado em sua correia.

– My nipple tassles seem to have become entangled in your thong.

É um homem ou mulher?

– Are you a man or a woman?

Enfim, nunca mente.Você vai fazer.

– Oh well, never mind. You'll do.

Nunca falam de uma vez mais isto.

– Never speak of this again.

From: Camilla Charmon [Camilla@Aylesburystables.com]
Sent: 10 September 2011 15:10
To: Orlando Charmon [thearchbishopofbanterbury@hotmail.com]
Subject: Re: Brazil!

Hello darling,

I'm glad you're having a lovely time in Brazil. We also visited some botanical gardens this weekend, it's so funny to think you were doing the same thing across the other side of the world! The artisanal market sounds lovely too, as does the hiking – I don't know how you packed it all in along with the carnival!

Anyway, your father says he'll transfer the funds tomorrow. He says you should have a report done at the police station. They won't catch the men who robbed you (there are probably knife-wielding maniacs stealing from people all the time over there) but it'll be useful to claim on the insurance. Maybe say they took your sunglasses too? It's always worth putting in a bigger claim while you're doing it.

Well, I've got to go. We've got three new horses at the stables and it's causing a real mess with the staff timetables – I think I'll have a riot on my hands! I hope Venezuela is nice, watch out for that Hugo Chavez though. Ghastly man.

Love,

Mum

PS. A letter came from UCAS today. Apparently the next deadline is approaching. We don't want a repeat of last time, do we?

Went lashing with Chavez. NBD.

Greetings from Venezuela

Hola! from Venezuela

News | Sport | Weather | iPlayer | TV | Radio | More ▾

BBC

NEWS LATIN AMERICA & CARIBBEAN

ome | World | UK | England | N. Ireland | Scotland | Wales | Business | Politics | Health | Education | Sci/Environment

frica | Asia-Pacific | Europe | Latin America | Middle East | South Asia | US & Canada

SOUTH AMERICA | Information and maps

Orders to invade Colombia only issued 'for the banter'

President Hugo Chavez today suffered a humiliating climbdown when he had to recall soldiers who officials say had been given orders 'by enemies'. At 03.00 a Presidential edict was issued from Miraflores palace, instructing Venezualan soldiers across the country to prepare for an invasion of Colombia 'for the banter'. This was followed by a series of orders of an increasingly surreal nature that have led many in the Venezuelan opposition once again to question the sanity of President Chavez. At 03.20, troops were ordered to 'get their balls out', then at 03.23 were told 'pint of miche: down or gay' and a missive was sent out to all garrisons to requisition 'dubstep' music, as 'it's not an invasion without dubstep'. Further oblique references came in one message that simply read 'ROFLMAO I'm literally the President', thought to be a coded message to Colombian rebels as well as an affirmation of Chavez's position against what he calls the 'propaganda of the elites' who assert that he is stifling democracy.

This morning there has been a sluggish reaction from Miraflores over this apparently abortive invasion. A clearly fatigued Chavez later appeared in his 'Hello President' talk show to accuse 'an infiltrating member of the hegemony of imperialists, the living personification of debauchery and Western moral erosion, and a kindred spirit of that drunken donkey George Bush', who Chavez claimed had sent out the messages after gaining access to his office. Rumours have swirled in Caracas about the identity of this person, with some Venezuelan military sources claiming that 'a Westerner wearing some kind of scarf' had commandeered the Presidential limousine before dumping it at the Colombian border. He is thought to either have been a member of the CIA or under the command of the Colombian government who have long sought to destabilise the Chavez regime. In the face of international condemnation, Chavez has been bullish, declaring that 'the oligarchy want us to live under the lash. We will not.'

There are liquor stores open at any hour where people can go and buy liquor. What is that? Is this a brothel or something? Venezuela is no brothel!
– President Hugo Chavez

Country no 7. COLOMBIA:

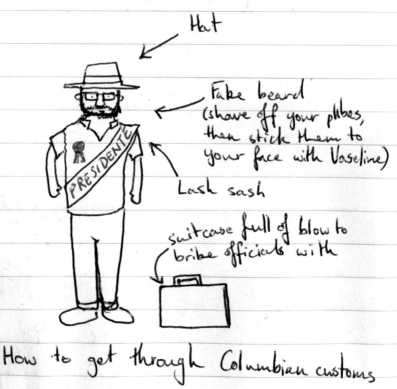

Didn't stay long in Colombia. Mostly as I was on the run from the government who thought I had tried to invade their country, and from the rebel FARC who were pissed off at me for not invading properly. Basically a massive mare, and this hangover has been world-ending. Literally like Alice in Chunderland this morning. There was even a rabbit bantering me. So, I may be unwelcome on this continent but on the plus side, I got a Medal of the Bolivarian Revolution and a Presidential sash as a bit of lash stash (and lash sash). I'd pretty much done South Americah anyway. Got the first flight I could out of Bogotá (luckily their customs officials are pretty incompetent) and now looking forward to having a chilled time in Australiah.

Hat

Fake beard
(shave off your phbes,
then stick them to
your face with Vaseline)

Lash sash

suitcase full of blow to
bribe officials with

How to get through Columbian customs

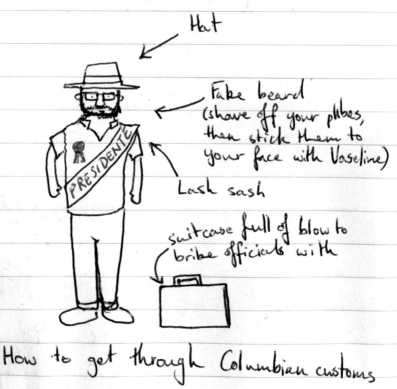

Oceania

Oceania
Notes:

Information and maps

Extra things to bring:

1. Sun cream — Usually I go without so that my skin can just man up, but they've got a hole in their ozone layer here. Sun cream is also useful for applying to your friend's back in the shape of a cock so that they're not only burned, but have a cock on them.

2. T-shirts with stupid slogans on — Australians are easily amused.

3. Your rugby boots — You'll probably have to play against the Fijians. Luckily they play sevens barefoot, so the studs can give you an advantage.

4. A plastic shark fin — Strap it on, go for a swim and scare some surfers. Best way to make friends.

5. Your pet frog — Ever since they deliberately introduced the cane toad to Australia, they've been keen to get more random additions to their ecosystem.

6. A massive knife — For killing crocodiles and shit.

7. A can of Fosters — to show Australians how bad the beer they export is.

Re-fill with wee
– see if they notice

8. An unhealthy disdain for aboriginal people. LOL.

35

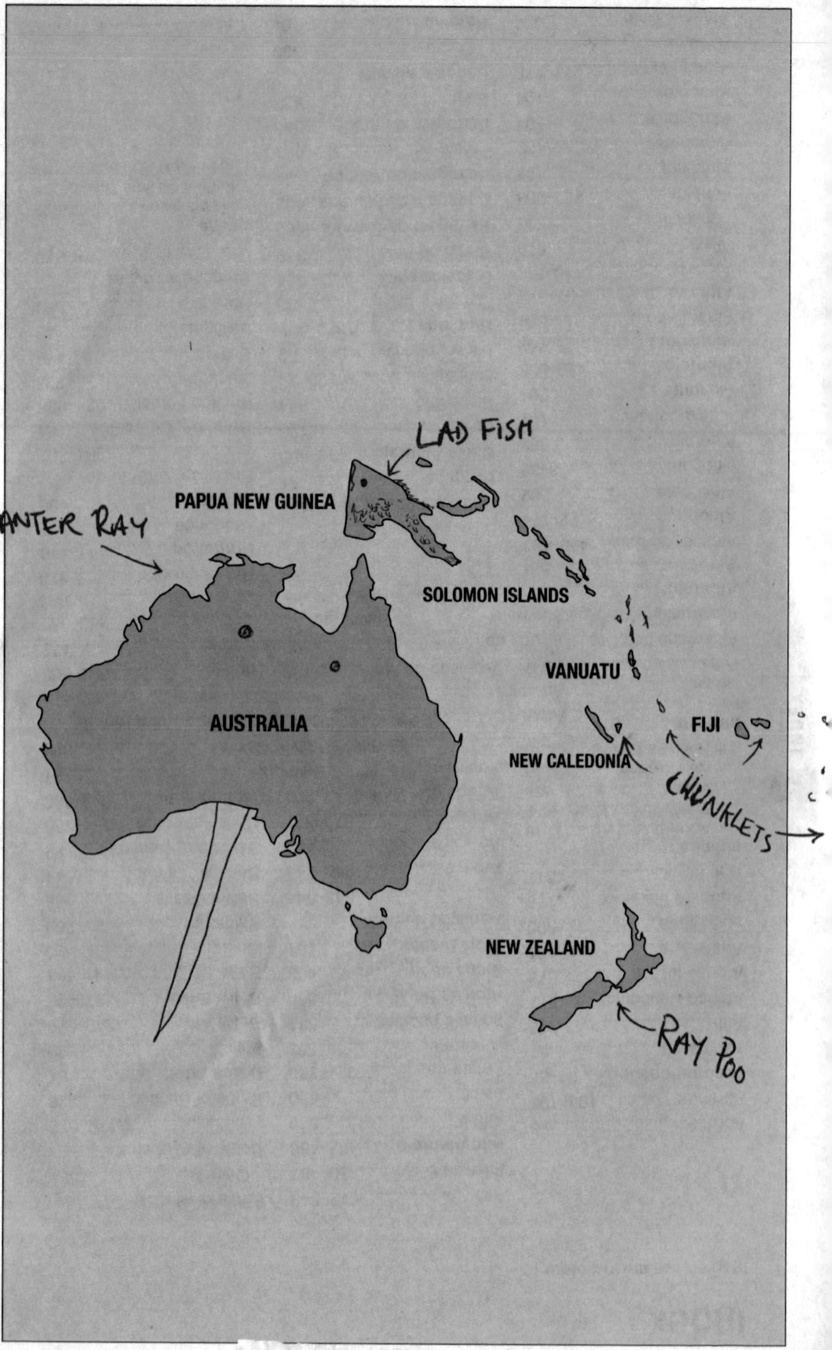

BANTER RAY

LAD FISH

PAPUA NEW GUINEA

SOLOMON ISLANDS

VANUATU

AUSTRALIA

NEW CALEDONIA

FIJI

CHUNKLETS

NEW ZEALAND

RAY POO

Country no 8. **FRENCH POLYNESIA:**

History of French Polynesia:

The island groups now known as French Polynesia were united in 1889 by the French
when they established a protectorate; they were first noticed by Europeans in 1521
when the Portuguese explorer Ferdinand Magellan sighted Pukapuka in the Tuamotu
Archipelago. Dutch explorer Jakob Roggeveen came across Bora Bora `. (so good_
`they named it twice!)` in the Society Islands in 1722, and the British explorer
Samuel Wallis was sent on an official mission to Tahiti in 1767 by King George III.
Wallis named the island of Tahiti 'King George III Island' and claimed it for England.

Shortly after, French navigator Louis-Antoine De Bougainville (`LAD Bougainville`)
landed on the opposite side of Tahiti and claimed it for the King of France.
Bougainville later wrote that the natives 'pressed us to choose a woman and come on
shore with her; and their gestures, which were not ambiguous, denoted in what
manner we should form an acquaintance with her'.
`I think this means doggy-style?`

France then used the island paradise as a nuclear-testing zone until 1996.
`Could make me glow in the dark! All over rave glow!`

Polynesian Culture:

The word 'tattoo' originated in Tahiti. The legend of Tohu, the god of tattoo, describes
painting all the oceans' fish in beautiful colours and patterns. `You should defo get
a tattoo here. I got the 'Mike Tyson'. Had to have it lasered
off my face fairly soon after, but it was so worth it ... When
I caught a fish, I gave it a tattoo that said 'Ladfish' just
to be cultural.`

Music and Dance

(From the Tahiti tourist board)

The beauty, drama, and power of today's Tahitian dance testify to its resilience in Polynesian culture. In ancient times, dances were directly linked to all aspects of life. One would dance for joy, to welcome a visitor, to pray to a god, to challenge an enemy, and to seduce a mate. `Got a bit mixed up with these. Ended up praying to an enemy, challenging a mate, welcoming a god and seducing a visitor.`

Language: *French Polynesia*

Ua poia poti marara – I'm on a boat.

JULIETTE

BIT OF A JAW!

Orlando's Diary: French Polynesiah

'Deep Blue She'

I'd been in Papeete for a few days and I was pretty bored, TBH. It was more Pizza Hut, than island paradise. Luckily for me, I'd put up a Facebook status saying 'I'm having an all-you-can-Papeete buffet!!' and a guy who was three years above me in school commented 'Dude, are you in Papeete??? I'm also there man!!!!' I didn't really know him very well - and he'd always seemed like a bit of a gimp - but then I didn't know anyone else around here, so I thought I may as well meet up with him?

We met up in a place called Le Piano Bar, which is French for a bar with a piano. This guy, Hugo, turned out to be decent enough (not premier league, but maybe he just needed some foreign investment), and we ended up getting fairly lashed. Hugo's out here on his year abroad from uni.* He decided to come out to Tahiti instead of 'going off to *gay* Paris like some kind of *gay* on a *school trip*, buddy'. Hugo is studying French at uni, so he's been able to get himself a job out here running a tourist boat, taking them to look at coral reefs and shit. At about 2 a.m., he was like, 'Maaaate, I gotta get some sleep - I'm running the boat tomorrow.' I obviously got on that bandwagon and asked if I could come. Told him I'd help him cook the lunch or something. He was a bit unsure, but I just bantered him into submission.

'OK pal, but you should probably get some sleep then too - it leaves at 8 a.m. sharp, with or without you.'

*note to self - apply for uni

He was still a bit of a loser, just like at school.

'I'll literally be there. Just gonna finish this cheeky beer. It'd be rude to leave just after Juliette bought me a drink.'

Juliette was just some random — I wasn't actually that bothered about being rude, she had a bit of jaw on her — but I wasn't going to go to bed just because a guy told me to. Anyway, I realised it would probably be easier to drink through, do an all-nighter and turn up on time at the beach absolutely Geoff Hooned.

It became increasingly apparent over the evening that 'Juliette' was actually a man in drag, particularly when she said she had been a drag act for several years and then performed in the bar beneath a banner reading 'Juliette is a man in drag'. Still, I kept her around and we drank through until the shops opened in the morning. She started getting a bit amorous, which I wasn't massively up for, so I said I had to go get my boat. Then, partly due to just wanting to fill a lull in conversation, and partly because I'd just seen a nice little floral swimming costume that would be very funny on her, I was just like, 'You can come too. I'm sure it'll be fine.'

So anyway, we turned up at the beach at 7.30 a.m. I saw Hugo, prepping the boat, which had a German family of four wearing matching bum-bags on board — he had clearly planned to leave without me, but I'd foiled his little plan by being too much of a lash hero. And, what's more, I'd brought a shemale. We jumped on the boat just as he was pulling away. He was all like, 'Oh, hey Orlando, you made it?!' and I was just like, 'Obv.'

'And who's this, chief?'

He was doing that thing that teachers do when they ask a question they already know the answer to.

'Juliette.'

He clearly didn't want me or Juliette there, but he had to pretend we were paying customers who had booked earlier, and the family who were bankrolling our jolly were staring at him and clearly very keen to get going.

It was probably about twenty minutes into the boat ride that I vommed. By then the excitement of being on a boat with a German family and a chick-with-a-dick had worn off. The motion of the boat was just a bit much for me after the all-night drinking, and

Juliette's tight-fitting new swimsuit meant I could see her plums bouncing up and down to the rhythm of the waves. She was wearing the swimsuit inside out, the gusset seams drawing the eye to places it didn't want to go. It all pretty much turned my stomach. The thing about vom is that the smell tends to set me off, and it turned out that it was the same for Juliette, who just launched a stream of Baxters extra chunky soup over the side of the boat. It's pretty difficult to withstand the sound and smell of people vomming either side of you but, to be fair, Hugo held himself together for a good ten minutes before a little chunklet appeared from his nose. He had been trying to hold it in but the pressure valve was open and he just erupted right onto the engine of the boat with one hand still on the tiller.

Turns out that emptying the contents of your stomach onto an engine isn't good for it, and after a bit of spluttering, it just gave out, chunderstruck.

We were there for about twenty minutes with Hugo apologising to the Germans (ironic!) and pulling the engine cord over and over again, getting exasperated to the point of tearful — but that may just have been vom-eyes. We weren't going anywhere. Hugo suggested that there were a lot of fishes and stuff, so we could just go snorkelling there, but understandably the Germans weren't too keen. Thing is, though, lots of other people were happy to get in, probably because they didn't know there was, like, stomach lining detritus and shit all round. One boat after another arrived and stopped next to us. One of the other boat guides said he had 'never seen such a concentration of Napoleon fish'!

I decided, fuck it, I'm getting in, so I did. It was literally amazing. I was surrounded by a myriad of coloured fish all jostling to sample the bounteous chunder, like a living tornado swirling around me and glinting with all the colours of the spectrum.

A giant manta ray had been attracted by all the commotion and swam over indolently. I hung out alongside that for a bit. It was really friendly; I named it Banter Ray.

I joined one of the other tourist boats when I came out of the water cos I was basically sick of looking at angry Hugo, miserable Germans and vacuum-packed gusset-junked Juliette. The other people didn't seem to mind me being there, or at least they didn't say anything, so I just fell asleep on their boat and before I knew it I was back in Papeete.

Country no 9. FIJI:

Official blurb from Fiji tourist board:

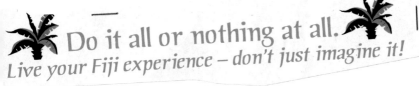

Do it all or nothing at all.
Live your Fiji experience – don't just imagine it!

To be fair, I once did imagine that I was in Fiji. I was actually in Tarquin's house, having passed out during a colonial-themed fancy dress party. Harry was dressed as a Nazi, as usual.

History of Fiji:

According to Fijian legend, the great chief Lutunasobasoba led his people across the seas to the new land of Fiji along with the snake god, Deigei, who had recently been spurned by a hawk who didn't want to hang out with him any more. Deigei then hatched some humans out of eggs and floated off with them to Fiji so they could populate the world. He apparently still lives in a cave and judges the souls of the dead, like a less serpentine version of Simon Cowell.

An advanced society had developed by the time Europeans accidentally stumbled upon the islands, and one not averse to cannibalism. This continued, despite the influence of missionaries, right up to the nineteenth century, with one chief, Ratu Udre Udre, reportedly eating over 872 people, each one marked by a stone that he would add to a pile.

Fijian Culture:

Food and Drink

Kava, the traditional drink of Fiji, has to be tried for the true Fijian experience. Made from the root of the pepper plant, traditionally this was prepared by virgins who chewed the root into a soft pulpy mass before adding water. Defo going to try this. Not sure why I need someone to chew for me, but I'm all for it. Mastication is literally boring.

Orlando's Diary: Fiji

'Fiji-ting'

I've been in Fiji for a few days, and already bought too much random crap. They're pretty hard-sellers here, and it's difficult to resist when you're all chilled out from drinking kava (Mummy was initially appalled that I was drinking kava until I explained it was a traditional drug-drink and not the champagne substitute). I've got a heap of necklaces and things that I'll have to offload on girls when I get back, but hopefully if I give them out to enough of the Cheltenham Ladies College crew, I'll get a return on my investment eventually. Blunderbuss approach. I also bought a traditional wooden canoe. The guy said he'd send it on, but I'm not entirely convinced.

***

Had a stroll down the King's Road on Viti Levu. At one point there was a pile of rocks next to a chieftain's grave. Apparently each rock represented someone that the chief had eaten. Apart from that, it's just like the King's Road in London, except no one seems to sell Crocs here.

***

I took a few trips out to the little islands and they were literally amazing, like sunsets that would make you properly spaff. On one of the Yasawa Island group I ran into Schalk, the boring Afrikaner I had met in South Americah. He was all like 'Bru, fokking fanny ti see you here. You should cime fir a game of rrrrugby. All the fokking guys from the hostel are. Don't worry, it's only touch – I know you nirthin himisphare buys get scared.'

So I ended up playing rugby – it was Fijians versus others and they literally bummed us. Beating the Fijians at rugby would have been like beating the French at being obnoxious (Clarkson-esque banter!); we were never going to do it. It didn't help that we had two Americans who kept throwing the ball forward even though we told them loads of times that it wasn't allowed. Anyway, it was still fun for a bit but it all turned a bit nasty when Schalk gouged one of the Fijian's eyes and we had to stop playing. I wandered off while everyone was shouting at each other and fell asleep on a beach.

NEW ZEALAND:

History of New Zealand:

The Dark Lord Sauron forged the One Ring to gain power over other rings held by the leaders of Men, Elves and Dwarves. He was defeated in battle, and Isildur cut off his finger, claiming the ring as a trophy of battle. Isildur, later overwhelmed by a band of Orcs, lost the Ring in the river Anduin. Fast-forward two thousand years and the Ring is found by the hobbit Sméagol on a fishing trip. He hides in the mountains and the Ring transforms him over the course of hundreds of years into a bizarre fish-man called Gollum. Eventually he loses the Ring, and it is found by Bilbo Baggins, who uses its power of invisibility to rescue his friends/go dogging. Meanwhile Sauron takes a new physical form and reoccupies Mordor, his old realm. Gollum sets out in search of the Ring, but is captured by Sauron, who learns that Bilbo has the Ring. Gollum is set loose, and Sauron, who needs the Ring to regain his full power, sends forth the Ringwraiths, who are a bit like the baddies in the Harry Potter Films, to seize it. Bilbo gives the ring to his nephew Frodo who takes it to Mount Doom and destroys it. The film then goes on for far too long about how happy everyone is in the Shire.

New Zealand Culture:

The *Haka* is a traditional Maori war dance that is performed by the New Zealand rugby team before they play. It takes many forms but at its most basic level the players put their left leg in, they put their left leg out, they do the hokey-cokey, then they turn around, and shout threats in Maori.

THREATENING TO FIST THE OPPOSITION. CLASSIC NEW ZEALAND.

Language: *New Zealand*

Bit of a dag – Comedian or joker.

Bludge – To sponge off others; as in 'dole bludger'.

Up the boohai shooting pukekos with a long-handled shovel – I'm just wandering around.

Give your ferret a run – Have sex.

Shufti – A look, as in 'Take a shufti at this, mate'.

Two sammies short of a picnic – Not the puffiest gilet in the cupboard.

Try to use all of these when you get back. When people ask you what the hell you're talking about, you can tell them it's the sort of shit they say out in NZ. And you know that because you went thah when you were up the boohai shooting pukkekos with a long-handled shovel. They'll probably feel two sammies short of a picnic when you point that out.

Orlando's Diary: New Zealand

'Bungee chump'

I've pretty much been airborne for most of my time in New Zealand. Everyone knows that it's the place to go to do all that adrenalin-junkie stuff. I wasn't that bothered about it, but I knew people'd be like, 'Oh, wow, you went to New Zealand, Flossie just came back from thah!' and then Flossie would be all like, 'Did you go bungee jumping too?' and then I'd have to make up stuff about bungee jumping because otherwise you look like a massive gimp. Much easier to just actually do it.

I got a flight over from Fiji to Auhckland then on to Queenstown – got it pretty cheap, but it turned out to have, like, hidden costs. I sat down, and I was just having a look at what in-flight booze I was going to get, when a massive lumbering frame plonked itself next to me. It was Schalk the South African, and he spent the next three hours boring the balls off me, talking about how 'shit the nirthin himisphere is'. A few gins eased the pain though, and by the end of the flight I actually started to warm to him, and found myself agreeing to join his bungee-jumping plan. It turned out we were staying at the same hostel again – I think we probably had the same guidebook? – and so once we were checked in, we hit the beers. Er, *hello* all-day drinking session, nice to see you, thanks for coming down ... Schalk taught me and some of the randoms we met at the hostel a drinking game called 'drink'. Essentially, you point at someone and shout 'Drink!' And they have to drink. I must have heard Schalk shout 'Draenk!' at me twenty times or something – he was like the verbal equivalent of a woodpecker — and the guys we were with, these Americans called Kurt, Randy and Steve, were raally getting into it. They thought this 'game' was the funniest thing they'd ever seen and they kept high-fiving each other as if the outcome was in any way surprising. By the time we hit some bars in town, everyone was pretty lashed, but the Americans were keen to hit it harder. 'No, fuck you, man. We're doing shots!!!'

The Americans were in bed by ten o'clock having massively overcooked themselves — I think they probably didn't drink often — and I was left with Schalk. 'Hey mun, those fokkin' Americans were pritty arrrogant, eh?' I was just like 'Yah' — I did remember Kurt claiming that Schalk was 'a pussy-O' and he would 'totally do him at bungee jumping'. Obviously for a South African to consider someone arrogant, they have to be raally running their mouths off.

'What tha fokk does "do him" mean? Sounds gauy, min.'
'Literally.'
(I didn't mention that he had probably learned the phrase from me ...)

'I'll fokking show him *who's* doing *who.*' Schalk said, pointing at the air.

He chilled out after a few more beers, and did his best to crack on to some Swedish birds by teaching them Afrikaans. He didn't really get anywhere, mostly because Afrikaans is probably the least sexy language in the world.

I woke up the next morning halfway up the stairs of the hostel. I had, like, decided that I couldn't be bothered to actually find my bed and that the stairs would do? It was a pretty all right place to sleep, except for the step imprint on my face from sleeping waardly. We were getting picked up to go bungee jumping in an hour, but I felt as rough as a two-dollar hooker (I think the Americans taught me that expression — it's pretty banterous!). I decided the only thing to do was pull the trigger and take a tactical, otherwise last night's dinner would come up on the jump. I was just doing that in the communal loos when Kurt, Randy and Steve came in. They were all like, 'Dude, that is fucking nasty' and Kurt was all 'Hello, I'm Orlando, I'm terribly nervous about bungee jumping. It's made me frightfully sick. I can't have my cup o' tea with the Queen.' Kurt was probably even more of a tool than I remembered.

We all got on the minibus that would take us to the bridge to jump off. It was being driven by an overly enthusiastic New Zealander. He was all up at the front of the bus squealing, 'Guys, you are going to have the experience of a lifetime. The ultimate adrenalin rush!!!!!'

Schalk just turned to me: 'Mun, I feel like shut.'

New Zealand whined on, 'And if any of you guys are feeling extra-adventurous, you can bungee jump *naked* for free!'

Kurt clearly thought this was a great idea. 'Hey Schalk, how about doing that if you're not *pussy*?'

'Fokk you, mun. I'll do it if you do.'

'Dude, naked bungee time!!!' Kurt exclaimed, high-fiving Randy.

Schalk looked as ill as I felt, and bungee jumping was blates the last thing he wanted to do, or probably the second last, after naked bungee jumping.

Kurt was now giving out massive chat about how he was going to do a swallow dive and that the skydiving instructor had said he was a natural because he showed no fear.

'I'm like a rock, man – no, I'm like *the* Rock.'

Schalk, for the first time I'd seen, was pretty quiet.

Before I knew it, we were in the queue, and Kurt was naked and having the harness attached. The guy was clearly pretty irked at having to bend down and fasten the harness with a cock in his face, probably made worse by the fact that he had to listen to Kurt's stinky chat.

'Man, I just wish we could make it actually scary.'

Once he was harnessed up, he turned to Schalk and said, 'Check out my swallow dive.'
Schalk said nothing.

As Kurt leaned forward into his jump, I just heard a voice: 'Wait! It's not attached!'

By that time, it was too late – Kurt had jumped. Just a split second before hearing of his impending death.

The bungee organiser suddenly went mental.

'Who said that? That's totally un-fucking-cool, mate. I hope the guy's OK.'

Schalk was unrepentant: 'That was fokking fanny, mun! Best joke I've ever done.'

They eventually pulled Kurt back up. Apparently the thought of his rope being unattached had caused him to pass out and shit himself on the way down. I'm not sure in what order, but I'm told they now sell DVDs of it from the booth on the bridge so you can decide for yourselves.

We stuck around long enough to see Kurt hauled up, shaking and covered in his own droppings, like a human skidmark.

Schalk went straight to the point: 'Hey mun, you're covered in shut.' Funny and true.

We decided to sack off the bungee jump and go for a cheeky beer to celebrate the fact that we weren't covered in poo. I didn't raally need to actually do a bungee jump now, as I got an anecdote anyway, and that's basically what it's all about.

From: David Charmon [charmond@parliament.uk]
Sent: 18 October 2011 14.21
To: Orlando Charmon [thearchbishopofbanterbury@hotmail.com]
Subject: Re: Noo Zealand

Dear Orlando,

Just a quick one – things are absolutely manic at my end. A colleague has put you on the salary to make geo-political briefings when you get back, but that's the last money you'll be getting out of me. It doesn't look good to have relatives on the payroll, so do try to be discreet …

I hope you enjoy New Zealand, and indeed Australia. I remember my time over there to watch the Ashes. Terribly funny – Kevin Rudd became so inebriated that he had to be carried to bed. A very weak drinker.

Have a great time, and be careful in Bangkok – I'm sure you know what I'm talking about. Best to wrap up at all times really, even with happy endings.

Best regards,
Pa

PS. That thing in Venezuela – nothing to do with you, was it?

PPS. Another letter from UCAS today. You said you'd apply online? I suggest you get your skates on – you don't want to end up in clearing doing 'David Beckham studies', do you?

PPPS. I know you're only spelling 'new' as 'noo' for a joke, but it isn't funny. Your generation uses far too much of this bloody 'text speak'.

PPPPS. Your cousin Jeremy showed me a picture of you on that face book thing. You appeared to have some kind of weird tattoo on your face. I hope for your sake that it isn't permanent. You looked like a total plank.

David Charmon
Member of Parliament for the constituency of Brigstocke-on-Wye
Chair, Standards and Privileges Select Committee

47

Country no 11. AUSTRALIA:

On satellite imagery Australia appears largely dry and barren. This is because it is largely dry and barren (70% arid or semi-arid), with a vast interior consisting of not one, but several, deserts. With geography not in their favour, Australian's have had to cultivate an almost pathologically optimistic sense of humour.

CHUNDER

While *chunder*'s etymology is often said to lie in the contraction of 'watch out under!', used in a naval context, its origins are in fact a lot more complex. Many have postulated that it comes from a series of advertisements for Blyth and Platt's Cobra boot polish which appeared in the *Bulletin* newspaper in Sydney from 1909 onwards, originally drawn by the well-known Australian artist Norman Lindsay. These featured a character named Chunder Loo of Akim Foo and were so popular that Norman's brother, Lionel Lindsay, wrote and illustrated *The Adventures of Chunder Loo* for Blyth and Platt in 1916. The character's name became a nickname in World War One (sometimes abbreviated to *Chunder*) – which is where the notion of a military link may have originated.

It's been suggested that the term is in fact rhyming slang (Chunder Loo = spew) and that it was first taken up by public schoolboys. It became surfing slang in the 1960s, and remains a particularly popular Australian word.

noun
1. *(context, Australian, slang)* vomit
verb *(chunders, chundering, chundered)*
1. *(context, Australian, slang)* to vomit.

Derivations: Chunderous, chundersome, chundertastic, chunderful, chunderlicious, chunderlier, chunderbus, chundercats, chunder milk wood.

History of Australia:

When Warlimpirrnga Tjapaltjarri first saw a European he said: 'I couldn't believe it. I thought he was the devil, a bad spirit, and was the colour of clouds at sunrise.'
`Note: Bring sun cream ...`

Initially discovered by Dutch explorers in 1606, Australia's east coast was claimed for Britain in 1770. During the eighteenth and nineteenth centuries, large numbers of convicts were brought to Australia after the revolutionary wars in America stopped those colonies being a destination for penal transportation.
`Penile transportation!!! LOL`

Australian Economics:

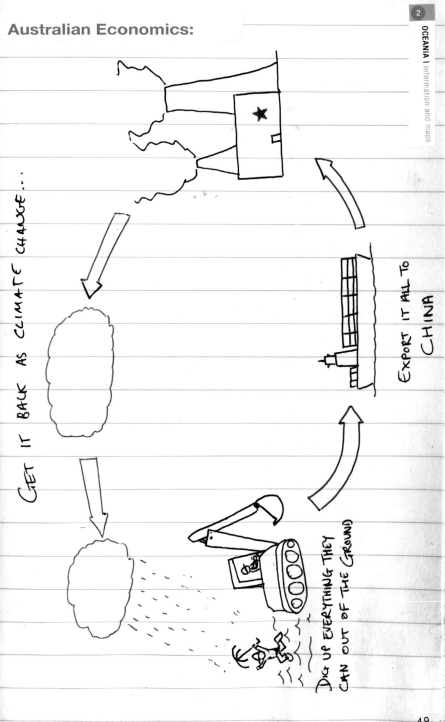

GET IT BACK AS CLIMATE CHANGE...

EXPORT IT ALL TO CHINA

DIG UP EVERYTHING THEY CAN OUT OF THE GROUND)

Australian Culture:

Australian Wildlife:

Australiah basically has loads of random animals that will kill you. These ones are the most dangerous:

ng san cre ioa

1. The Box Jellyfish

One of the most lethal animals in the world; stings are extremely painful and cause death in most instances. Vinegar is the most effective palliative for the stings, but urine will also have some effect and could be a good excuse to indulge your bizarre fantasies with a consenting adult.

SHAME IT'S SO DANGEROUS, OTHERWISE IT WOULD MAKE THE MOST BANTEROUS HAT IN THE WORLD — CRAZY GLOW-IN-THE-DARK DREADLOCKS PERFECT FOR RAHVING.

2. The Taipan

The Taipan is found throughout Australia and is both large and fast, in addition to having the most toxic venom of any terrestrial snake species worldwide. Extreme care should be taken when walking through sugar fields where it is often found hunting rats. Taipans usually stay away from people but once cornered or threatened, they will strike multiple times. *MY SNAKE STRIKES MULTIPLE TIMES TOO! BUT ONLY WHEN CORNERED...*

3. Saltwater Crocodile

Saltwater crocodiles are the largest reptiles in the world and can grow up to 18 feet (5.45 metres) in length. Found in Thailand, Vietnam and Northern Australia they present a danger not only to humans but even to animals as large as water buffalo. Their 'death roll', where they grab prey and roll continuously until it dies, is, as you might expect, particularly deadly.

The only protection against this fearsome predator is the traditional Australian method of tying corks to your hat.

4. Blue-ringed Octopus

The blue-ringed octopus is one of the most toxic creatures the ocean has to offer, made even more dangerous by its small size (comparable to a golf ball). Its potent venom has no known antidote. *BET IT'S TASTY IF YOU BATTER IT THOUGH...*

BANTER!

5. Stone Fish

Difficult to see owing to the fact that it looks like a stone (as the name suggests), this is the most venomous fish in the world, living camouflaged on the bottom of reefs. Its dorsal area is lined with thirteen venomous spines,which can cause shock, paralysis and tissue death depending on the severity of the sting.

YOUR MUM.

6. Redback Spider

The redback spider is notorious for apparently hiding under Australian toilet seats and has thus taken its place in the panoply of creatures that can kill you on this continent. Its neurotic venom induces severe pain, so try to avoid using any toilets in Australia. It is also one of the few spider species that displays sexual cannibalism while mating. *JUST LIKE FULHAM GIRLS!!!*
ROFLcopter.

7. Russell Crowe

Usually found dwelling in the bars or nightclubs of Sydney, this chameleonic predator is just as much at home in an ancient Roman colosseum as an American university. Particularly dangerous when cornered, this creature should be approached with extreme caution, especially when brandishing a weapon such as a telephone.

8. Tiger Snake

Yet another venomous snake? Yep. And with a mortality rate of around 45% on untreated bites, it's another to be extremely wary of. In addition the species is protected in most states and any harming or injuring leads to a fine of up to $4,000. So it's a danger not just to your health, but also to your wallet.

9. Great White Shark **(Australian pronunciation: Shaaaaaaaaaaaaaaaaaaaaaaaaaark)**

This exceptionally large shark is the world's best-known predatory fish. Sharks – despite Spielberg's hateful propaganda – do not actually target humans as prey and as such many attacks aren't fatal, with the shark only performing 'test-bites' out of curiosity. Like a child gnawing their expensive new gift. Humans simply aren't a good meal, considering the shark's slow digestion and a human's muscle-to-fat ratio.

ONLY DANGEROUS IF YOU'RE A MASSIVE FATTY THEN —
WATCH OUT TARQUIN'S MUM!

10.

10. DUCK-BILLED
PLATYPUS

I TRIED TO SNEAK A DUCK-BILLED PANTERPUS BACK WITH ME, BUT IT STUNG ME WHEN I TRIED TO PUT IT IN MY SUITCASE (HOW DOES SOMETHING THAT LOOKS LIKE A CROSS BETWEEN A BEAVER AND A DUCK PRODUCE VENOM?! WTF?!). LITERALLY WELL SORE. PEOPLE SAID IT WASN'T ANYWAH NEAR 'TOP TEN MOST DANGEROUS' BUT I'VE PUT IT IN AT NUMBER TEN BECAUSE I KNOW BETTER.

39. CRAZY BARRY'S

CRAZY BARRY'S is an iconic Sydney bar. The party never stops here, despite local councillors' complaints!! And you'll find that this legendary venue is still rockin' the free world! Its happy hour lasts five hours and if you're feeling adventurous, ask for a Pom-nailer, a drink so alcoholic it makes your eyeballs hurt.

SPENT AGES TRYING TO FIND THIS PLACE BUT APPARENLY IT CLOSED LIKE THREE YAHS AGO!? <u>BULLSHIT.</u>

Crazy Barry's

...Still rockin' the free world!

Happy hour 7pm - 12AM!

VEGEMITE:
A SPREAD FOR
TOAST THAT
TASTES EVEN
WORSE THAN
MARMITE. THE
CULINARY
EQUIVALENT
OF A YEAST
INFECTION.

Orlando's Diary: Australiah

'Land down chunder'

Australiah has basically been
massively chilled. Just been
surfing, hanging out on the
beach, and doing cultural pursuits
like drinking beer through a funnel,
vomiting, drinking beer through a funnel, vomiting,
repeating ad nauseam.

Everyone I was travelling with got jobs in bars here in
Sydney. At first I didn't, as I'm not sure work is
raally my thing, but then I realised that being in a bar
was my thing, and it was sooo easy to get a job as all
their bar staff have gone to Fulham. Which is probs
literally ironic. Schalk got a job in a South-African
bar across the road from my one, so I would often see
him shouting things and setting fire to drinks through
the window.

　　　　One day we were on our afternoon break and
decided to wander down to the beach to eat some ice
cream (life is sooo hard!! LOL). We were just wandering
around by the seafront when we saw a guy with a
sandwich board that said 'Vietnamese out', probably
promoting a restaurant or something. Schalk was just
like, 'Mun, actually I wuld fokking demolish some
noodles right now.' We asked the guy whah the restaurant

was, but he wasn't helpful at all. There was a guy doing burgers there though, so we got a burger and went to eat it on the beach.

After a few weeks of working in the bars we quit. I had had enough of it anyway as it was literally slave labour, and Schalk had 'set fire to one too many customers for his job to be viable'.

Sydney had been great bants, but obviously there was a lot more of Australiah that we hadn't seen, so we decided that the best way to remedy that was to join a bus tour that would visit various other places. Apparently the locals call it 'the fuck truck', so you know it's good. And it was pretty massive (although not literally as there were only 32 seats). It was the four B's: Beach, Booze, Banter, Bees. I mean the bees weren't that positive, cos I got stung, but all the rest was A-MAZE.

At this club in Byron Bay I had a bit of a revelation. I looked across the bar of Cheeky Monkeys' and Schalk was shouting at some girl he had inadvertently set fire to through a badly executed flaming sambucca. The bar smelt of burnt hair. I realised at that point that I was probably not making many new friends by hanging around with Schalk, so I decided to drop him and travel solo. I obviously didn't tell him that, I just stopped going to the first place my guidebook recommended. It's actually pretty easy to lose people when you're travelling.

Now just chilling on a beach — there's a guy playing guitar, which would be quite pleasant if he wasn't so literally annoying. The only problem with Australiah is that there are a lot of these budget James Blunts walking around. It's like a biblical plague. People gather around them to sing along but then they do an obscure Jack Johnson song so they can sing on their own. Literally show-offs. And they're all called Tom and come from Cheltenham and have floppy hair. Schalk told me that he once put one of their guitars in a bonfire 'because the goy jist wuldn't shut the fokk up.' I kinda miss him. He was obviously a bit of a tool, but he had his moments. That's the problem with travelling: you make fleeting acquaintances, and enjoy experiences that are inherently transient. It's like what Caesar said: Veni, Vidi, Vomui.

Country no 12. PAPUA NEW GUINEA:

Official advice from Papua New Guinea Tourist board:

Q: *Is it safe to come to Papua New Guinea?*

A: Papua New Guinea is filled with friendly people and lovely smiles although common sense must prevail.

Language: *Papua New Guinea*

Over 800 languages are spoken in Papua New Guinea.

JUST SPEAK ENGLISH HERE, UNLESS YOU WANT TO BOTHER LEARNING A LANGUAGE THAT ONLY ABOUT TEN PEOPLE SPEAK. MAYBE YOU'LL DO THIS IF YOU'RE WELSH...

Orlando's Diary: Papua New Guinea
'Papua's New Guinea Pig'

I was going to head off into the jungle to banter some tribes that have never met any Westerners. I thought I could give them my old iPhone just to shit up some anthropologists when they came to 'discover' them. Then someone told me that some of the indigenouses are still, like, cannibals so I stayed urban as I'm pretty awah that I have a tasty-looking rump. Massively not up for being eaten, except in the euphemystical way. Boom.

The hostel I was staying in Port Moresby was pretty well-placed, but I can't remember the name of it and, TBH, you probably

57

wouldn't want to stay there because of the owners, who were
pretty waard. When I came to check in the guy was thah in a
string vest. He had one of those guts that just seem to come
from nowhere, like he was properly preg, and he was resting
this sizeable belly on the check-in desk. I told him I had a
reservation, and he just said: 'My concubine will show you to
your room.' I stood there for a bit looking at him, expecting
something to happen, until he motioned downwards with his eyes
and there was a very small woman eyeing me expectantly and
wiping her mouth. She then went off down the corridor and it
was clear she wanted me to follow. When we got to the room she
pointed me to the bottom bunk nearest to the door, which I
thought was a bit waard as like there weren't any other people
in the dorm, but I figured they'd probably arrive later (I
usually choose the top bunk, ever since Tarquin told me about
the time the guy above him pissed himself — literally not keen
on getting a golden shower from a stranger). Being pretty
knackered from travelling, I decided to get an early one so
that I could have my lash hat on the next day.

I was awoken by a bit of light spilling in from the doorway,
until most of it was blocked out by a sizeable silhouette. I
could tell from the outline of the swollen gut that it was the
hostel guy. I figured he probably wanted to rape me or rob me
or something so I played at being asleep, but I knew I had a
traditional spear in my bag if any shit kicked off. What I
massively hadn't clocked was the little woman, who by this time
was right on top of me, literally. I felt her hands touching
me through the sheet and she just kept sniffing me. Then, with
one final sniff of my face and some bizaarre loud breathing,
they were both gone. Fucking waard. Cheap hostel though, so
swings and rahndabouts.

NOT TO BE CONFUSED WITH CONCUBINE
UNLESS IT'S A PORCUPINE CONCUBINE

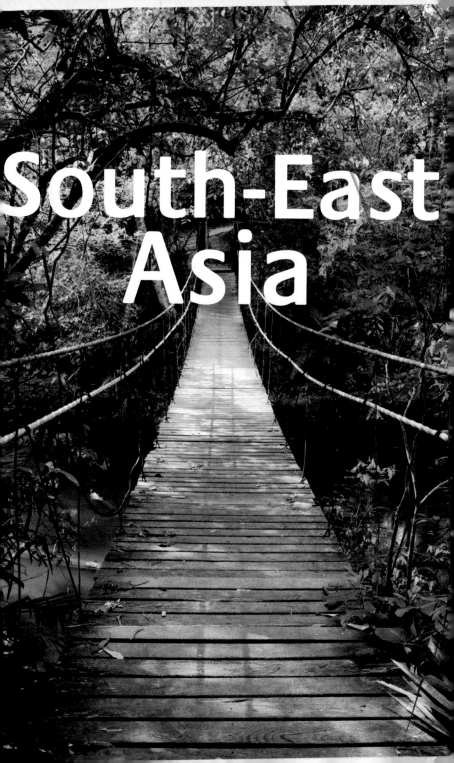

South-East Asia

South-East Asia
Notes:

ℹ️ Information and maps

South-East Asiah is basically whah we all go. It's as much of
a rite of passage as a game of soggy biscuit or buying your
first Jack Wills gilet. Before I went, I felt like I already
knew the place — I'd grown up hearing stories from people in
the years above me about how a guy called Bozzer had thought
he was a crocodile for three days after taking some crazy
shit, and Xavier de Toulis had accidentally donkey-punched a
prozzer in Bangkok. I wanted to do all of it — until I found
out what some of it actually was (I was still pretty young).
Then I wanted to do most of it. My travels here were literally
following in the footsteps of giants.

Things you don't need to bring:

1. Valium — You can get it in chemists here.

2. Branded items — This is the best place to pick up
   knock-off stuff, so any real stuff will look fake.

3. Tailored suits — While you're here you can get a
   raally cheap suit made. The stupider the better.

4. Landmines — They've already got plenty over here.
   If anything, they have too many.

5. Orchids — They're raally cheap here. They get a bit
   squashed in your bag though. Not sure why you'd want
   them in the first place either.

6. Gold, jewellery and gems — Stuff here is so cheap
   that you could dress up like a bling Henry VIII for,
   like, a tenner or something.

7. Inappropriate or nonsensical English-language novelty
   slogan T-Shirts — They're big over here.

8. Respect for the law — That only inhibits your fun.

9. A statue of the Buddha — Again, they've already got
   plenty. If anything, too many.

10. A guidebook — You can pick them up over here
    for a fraction of the price. You're literally
    a mug if you buy a guidebook in the UK.

You
↙

Country no 13. INDONESIA:

Indonesia is the world's largest archipelagic state, home to the world's largest Muslim population as well as being the world's third largest democracy. Essentially there are a lot of people in Indonesia, spread over 17,508 islands (6,000 inhabited). I'm probably only going to one — Bali. Although, if there are loads .. uninhabited, maybe could buy one? Could make myself a king?

An average tourist spends $100 per day in Bali compared to the local daily spend of just $2. Luckily, I'm not an average foreign tourist. Live like a local, drink like a foreign.

Indonesia is home to the 35-centimetre-high miniature deer. Miniature venison!!! The Indonesian archipelago also provides the natural habitat for a species of fish that climbs trees to catch insects as well as spiders that use their webs to catch small birds for their dinner. When I first saw these weird animals, I initially thought I was hallucinating. When I also decided I was made of concrete, I realised I actually was! ROFLMAO!

Indonesia sits on the Pacific 'ring of fire' leading to regular volcanic eruptions, earthquakes and tidal waves.

RULES TO 'RING OF FIRE'

- Get a pack of cards and spread them in a circle around an empty pint glass.
- Take it in turns to pick up a card. Each card has a different forfeit — these will change depending on who you're playing with but these are the ones we played while on the Pacific ring of fire, so they're obviously right.

Card forfeits:

Ace = *Waterfall:* You drink for as long as the person to your right does.

2 = *Nominate:* You choose who must drink.

3 = *Me:* You drink.

"RING OF FIRE"
RULES CONT...

4 = *Drink while you think*: The Name Game (See Appendage for rules)

5 = *Play fives*: See Appendage for rules

6 = *Bombmaster*: Someone shouts 'Bomb!' and the last person to hit the floor has to drink (this was always a bit of an edgy one to play in Bali)

7 = *Categories*: Think of a category and go around the circle saying stuff from that category until someone gets it wrong

8 = *Mate*: Choose someone to drink with you.

9 = *Rhyme*: Go around the circle saying things that rhyme with a word — e.g. punt, runt, gunt

10 = *Tarquin*: Make Tarquin drink for being such a shit lad. If he's not actually playing, you have to ring him and make him drink whatever's nearest to him (last time it was gravy).

Jack = *Invent a rule*: You make up a rule and everyone has to follow it — e.g.: For the rest of the game, replace the word 'beer' with 'Tarquin is a bender'

Queen = *21s*: See Appendage for rules

King = *Fill cup*: When you get a king, you pour your drink into the central cup. The last person to pick a king has to drink the horrible mixture.

Joker = Just make up a forfeit for this card if you have it — e.g.: For the rest of the game, replace the word 'drink' with 'Tarquin is a bender'

NB. Ring of Fire is best played with novelty playing cards, like animals of the forest or shemale porno ones.

Language: *Indonesia*

Tante Girang – A woman who likes to have sex with a younger man, lit. means 'happy auntie'.

TOP TIP: Get yourself a Tante Girang if you're short of monies.

Sloaney Planet Recommends:

47. THE GILGAMESH

THE GILGAMESH is probably the most fun place this reviewer has ever been to. With cocktails flowing due to an unexpected free tab and a great party atmosphere, the Gilgamesh should not be missed.

WENT THAR— IT WAS SHIT. HAD THE REVIEW IN THE WINDOW, AND LOADS OF PEOPLE WITH THIS GUIDEBOOK INSIDE, ALL LOOKING CONFUSED AS TO HOW THEY'D BEEN LURED IN.

Orlando's Diary: Indonesyah

'It burns, burns, burns'

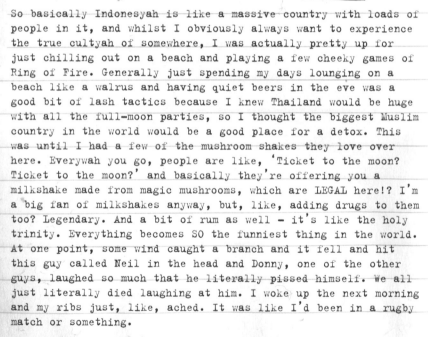

So basically Indonesyah is like a massive country with loads of people in it, and whilst I obviously always want to experience the true cultyah of somewhere, I was actually pretty up for just chilling out on a beach and playing a few cheeky games of Ring of Fire. Generally just spending my days lounging on a beach like a walrus and having quiet beers in the eve was a good bit of lash tactics because I knew Thailand would be huge with all the full-moon parties, so I thought the biggest Muslim country in the world would be a good place for a detox. This was until I had a few of the mushroom shakes they love over here. Everywah you go, people are like, 'Ticket to the moon? Ticket to the moon?' and basically they're offering you a milkshake made from magic mushrooms, which are LEGAL here!? I'm a big fan of milkshakes anyway, but, like, adding drugs to them too? Legendary. And a bit of rum as well — it's like the holy trinity. Everything becomes SO the funniest thing in the world. At one point, some wind caught a branch and it fell and hit this guy called Neil in the head and Donny, one of the other guys, laughed so much that he literally pissed himself. We all just literally died laughing at him. I woke up the next morning and my ribs just, like, ached. It was like I'd been in a rugby match or something.

I didn't really see much of Indonesia because I was too busy chilling in Bali — felt like such a tourist!! But, you know, sometimes you want to. I even bought one of those Bintang beer wife-beaters like all the Americans here. I love *Anchorman* catchphrases as much, in fact much more, than the next man, but

I've literally been hearing them call their arms 'guns' every five minutes. Like OMG, get some new catchphrases! Not to be racist or anything, but Yanks can be pretty dumb …

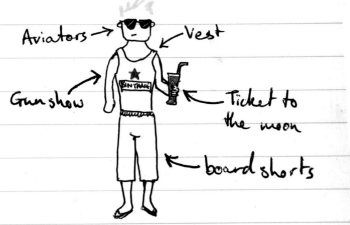

Aviators → ← Vest

Gun show → ← Ticket to the moon

← board shorts

Played a lot of Ring of Fire while I was here, and as I left I even saw a group of people I didn't know playing it — they all follow whatever 'the big deal' does. (People started calling me that because 'I'm a kinda big deal', obv.)

I was hanging around with a 'mature backpacker' called Julie for a bit in Bali. She was fairly good banter, especially the way she would, like, pay for stuff, but she got annoying after a while. She had apparently been a banker before she lost her job and decided to go travelling. Blah blah hedge fund … subprime whine whine. I obviously couldn't give less of a shit, but she kept arguing with the hippies about capitalism, as if she really cared what they said. The thing about meeting people when you're travelling is that it's not usually worth having massive arguments, and hippies are obviously raally spiritual so you should listen to their views about, like, transcengenital stuff, but generally you shouldn't take economic advice from anyone who doesn't wash their hair and shits in a bucket, so there's no point getting into a fight about capitalism. Julie kept going on about how I knew nothing about the real world, which I thought was pretty stupid. Especially coming from someone who was about to go off and join some commune that she had seen in Eat, Pray, Love. Basically, old people just shouldn't go backpacking. It's like Facebook, they just don't understand it — they just spend their whole time on FarmVille. And in that metaphor, FarmVille stands for talking shit with hippies and annoying me. Long story short, I cut her loose and headed off for Malaysiah.

Country no 14. **MALAYSIA:**

Didn't stay long — Cash-lash ratio not great.

GUIDING PRINCIPLE

Country no 15. **THAILAND:**

Thailand's 'cool season' runs from November until the end of February. This is the best time to visit as the humidity and heat are lower, although it is not actually 'cool' in British terms (but then you're in Thailand, so I don't know why you'd expect it to be!). Obviously, as it's the best time to come, more people do, so resorts get much busier.

You'll probably fly into Bangkok, but if you're not just here for sex tourism or to get mashed on a beach, you may want to visit Chiang Mai, the most culturally significant city in northern Thailand, to see the numerous significant religious sites or even to learn traditional Thai cooking. Visitors are particularly recommended to see Wat Phrathat Doi Suthep, the city's most famous temple, which stands on Doi Suthep, a hill to the north-west of the city, and dates from 1383. Its site is said to have been chosen by placing a relic of the Lord Buddha on an elephant's back and letting it wander around until it trumpeted, circled and died (obviously next to an elephant corpse is the best place to build a temple). The temple's location provides superb views on a clear day. But you've probably stopped reading by now, so let's talk about Bangkok, ladyboys and ping-pong ball shows.

Bangkok in numbers:

Official Name: Krung Thep Mahanakhon Amon Rattanakosin Mahinthara Ayuthaya Mahadilok Phop Noppharat Ratchathani Burirom Udomratchaniwet Mahasathan Amon Piman Awatan Sathit Sakkathattiya Witsanukam Prasit. That's more of a mouthful than you'd get at your average Thai sex show ...

Population: 6.9 million (city); 11.5 million (metropolitan)

Average Winter Temperature: 26°C / 79°F / **Average Summer Temperature:** 29°C / 84°F

Number of monks in Thailand: 200,000

Number of ladyboys: 200,000 (statistic not verifiable)

Thailand holds the Guinness world record for the longest condom chain.

Key fact: Bangkok is sinking at the rate of 5cm per year. Some say this is a slow re-run of Noah's flood. Others say this is a re-run of Sodom and Gomorrah.

MONEY-SAVING TIP: Sex bars make money by exploiting the desires of their customers. For some reason, most of the sex bars in Bangkok have board games in them. Don't get drawn in to betting on competitive games of Connect 4 against hookers. They're really good at it. They're just hustling you.

Also, wine is considered a 'luxury good' and therefore taxed at 160%. Cash-lash ratio is consequently poor. Drink something else.

Language: *Thailand*

Mao sut – Lit. 'drunk animal', used to describe someone who is extremely intoxicated.

Sohpaynee – Prostitute (lit. beautiful woman).

Khun toi – Prostitute.

Dok thong – Prostitute.

Pooching – Camp gay guy/tranny.

Gig – Secret lover/sex slave.

Farang – White-looking person.

Orlando's Diary: Thailand

'Elephant Men'

I arrived in Bangkok and basically had a mental one right from stepping off the plane. Tarquin, Radleigh and Pharoah (his parents own half of Egypt so we call him Pharoah – can't actually remembah his real name at this point) had decided to meet me there, so, with these three chunder monkeys in tow, I hit the town. First off, went to one of those MBK centres to pick up knock-off stuff. Got a raally cheap-looking Rolex for my old man. He'll hate it – he's big on, like, copyright and all that shit. He's literally medieval – probably even still pays for music and porn …

So, people always go on about the ping-pong ball shows here, but what they don't mention is all the non-ping-pong ball stuff. For a start, Tarquin has refused to use his iPad ever since. At one point, she even shoved a paintbrush up there and did a portrait of me. I think I'll turn it into a postcard and send it to my old man. Radleigh got hit in the face with a banana projectile too. Newton's laws of motion are all put to good effect here. For every action, there is an equal and opposite rim-action.

Because all the sex bars are in the same place, you can go to loads without really noticing, except that your money diminishes. After a while, you see so much flesh that you forget that women usually wear clothes. It's a bit like that film, *Alien*, in that stuff just keeps popping out of places, and it gets less and less surprising.

After one massive night out in Bangkok, I woke up and my world was moving. I was asleep on a plank, looking up at the sky. At first I thought I was on a boat, because of the rocking, but it just didn't smell right for a boat, which sounds a bit waard. Suddenly, I heard Pharoah's voice: 'Look, a fucking tiger! Who's got the camera?' I got up, and at that point I realised I was on an elephant. We couldn't find the camera in time, and the tiger just wandered off. After a while we reached a village, got off the elephant and tied it to a post so we could have a beer in a little shack.

'Tarquin, wah did we get the elephant?'

'Oh yah, elephant.' Tarquin still had a glazed look, so I asked Pharoah.

'Literally no idea. Maybe we nicked it?'

'Best lash stash evah!'

'Could've swapped it for the camera?'

'Elephant's worth more than a camerah, though.'

'Oh yah. Maybe not over here though. Over here, they're like cows.'

'Oh yah, cows.'

'Wah's Radleigh?'

'Don't know. Wah are we?'

'Literally no idea.'

'Wah did we get these suits from?' (We were all wearing matching bespoke pink satin suits for some reason.)

'No idea. They're good though.'

'I look like Jonathan Ross ...'

'Banter!'

Then Tarquin got sick on his shoes and the woman who ran the shack threw us out. When we got back to wah we had tied up the elephant, it was gone. Don't know whether it had just gone off on its own, been nicked, or the owner had come and got it – either way, we probs should have tied it up tighter. There weren't any taxis around, cos it was, like, a village, and no one wanted to talk to us (mostly cos of Tarquin, who looked a bit mental ...). We asked about Bangkok and a guy said it was in the direction we had come from, which, like, made sense. So we just set off walking, the whole way back properly shitting ourselves about the fact that there was obviously a tiger around somewah. Pharoah was nearly crying by the time we reached a town we could tuk-tuk from. Such a gayer.

Lash heroes

Elephant

Still, we made it back to Bangkok without being eaten. Have that, so-called king of the beasts! 1-0!

Radleigh was already at the hotel when we arrived back.
        'Bonjour knob-jockeys! Wah've you been?'
        'On an elephant.'
        'Mental.'
        'Wah wah you?'
        'Guys, I've got some banter for you, but you literally can't tell anyone else.'
        'Literally.'
        'So, like, I lost you guys at some point after the karaoke bar, and went on a solo mission. Had a million beers and basically got a prozzer. Went back to hers, did the business, passed out in her bed. Musta been immovable - I was so lashed, and proper knackered. Anyway, when I woke up in the morning, I could see this thing curled up at the end of the bed. It was like, her kid. Pretty waard. Didn't stay long after that. Made the morning blowie-j pretty edgy too.'

After Bangkok, we went to Ko Panang to the full-moon party. Pretty average raally. The pre-parties were better than the main event, and there were too many Etonians thah. So annoying. Also, went to the beach from *The Beach*. Not great either. Probs shouldn't go to places that a book tells you to. Had plenty of Chang beer, and a few pretty serious 'Changovers'…

Everyone at the full-moon party was covered in cuts from falling over stuff and stepping on glass. One guy, Rob, from Newcastle, had to have a toe amputated cos a cut had gone septic in some dirty water. Tarquin asked him a question that he didn't know the answer to and I was like 'that's *stumped* you'. Nearly got in a fight over that, but it was worth it for the punnage.
        Radleigh was picking up girls by hanging around with some bandages and anti-septic, playing Florence Nightingale, all like caring and shit. Apparently he was 'well in with a fit burn-victim' until some bird with a shattered pelvis cock-blocked him by calling an ambulance for herself and the burn-girl. I don't know what I took that night, but I could hear techno music in my head for like three days. Pretty annoying. Also, Tarquin got attacked by some stray dogs and has started foaming at the mouth.

PORTRAIT OF ME
FROM PING-PONG
BALL SHOW.
OBVIOUSLY IT'S NOT VERY
GOOD, BUT TO BE FAIR,
SHE DID DO IT WITH
HER VAG.

Country no 16. CAMBODIA:

History of Cambodia:

According to myth, Cambodia came into being through the union of an Indian Brahmin named Kaundinya and the daughter of a dragon king. Kaundinya was apparently sailing past her father's kingdom when she paddled out to greet him. Not used to people being friendly, Kaundinya shot her boat with an arrow, which scared her so much that she agreed to marry him. However, she didn't have enough money for a dowry, so naturally her father chose to suck all the water out of his kingdom as a wedding gift. It was said to be something of an awkward present and ended up just being put in storage.

`Best way to pull in Cambodia - shoot arrows at women ...`

Cambodians later established the sizeable Khmer empire, conquering a substantial portion of South-East Asia in the process. The temple created at the heart of this empire, Angkor Wat, the eighth wonder of the world, still stands as a testament to the influence of the Khmers. As the empire declined in strength, Cambodia lost territory to both the Thais and the Vietnamese, and it seemed as if it would be subsumed into one or both neighbouring states until the Cambodian king invited the protection of the French from its aggressors. In 1863, it became a French protectorate. During WWII, as France was conquered by the Germans, it wasn't able to protectorate anyone else, so Cambodia came into Japanese hands. `Wahey!`

During the Vietnam War, Cambodia suffered widespread bombing from the USA who were trying to disrupt the supply lines of the Vietcong operating there.

Some commentators see this as having helped the rise of the communist Khmer Rouge to power. In pursuit of a rural utopia, Pol Pot's Khmer Rouge abolished money and private property. They forced city dwellers to move to rural areas and work the fields – the effects of which can still be seen today, with around 70% of Cambodia's workforce employed in subsistence farming. `So authentic-organic farming.`

Pol Pot's 'cleansing' of the country resulted in the death of between 1.7 and 2.5 million people

`Guidebooks can really bum you out sometimes ...`

Cambodian Culture:

Food and Drink

There's a selection of traditional South Asian fare on offer in Cambodia, but for the more adventurous, the array of deep-fried insects are a must. Battered tarantula is considered a particular delicacy in some areas! Cambodians are similar to the Scottish in that they will pretty much batter anything.

Prahok should also be sampled while in Cambodia; it's a grey foodstuff made from gutted, mashed, fermented fish. You can eat this fermented fish paste raw, cooked, as a dipping sauce, and as a crucial ingredient in many typical Khmer foods. It's like a national icon, so much so that some men select their wives based on their ability to make fish paste. I COD FIND MY SOLE MATE IN CLAMBODIAH! (FISHBANTS...)

Orlando's Diary: Cambodiah

KALASHNIKOV!!

'The Lives of Udders'

Went to Angkor Wat (temple from *Tomb Raider*). Actually pretty impressed despite massive temple fatigue. Made the mistake of going to another one in Phnom Penh after. So bored. I know it's raally spiritual, but OMG how many statues of the Buddha do you actually need? He's pretty much just doing the same thing in all of them.

Also, Tarquin has had to go home as he's got rabies. Such a weak lad.

***

Went on a history tour while I was here. Literally learnt more in a day than the whole of school, and they didn't even give us coursework. Saw the mountain of skulls in the killing fields. The brutality of the torture and killing by the Khmer Rouge raally hit me and I was just, like, overwhelmed by man's inhumanity to man.

At the end of the historical tour of the killing fields we went to a range and played at firing AK47s. A lot of people were all like 'Ooh I don't feel like it any more', and TBH I had this feeling at the bottom of my stomach that I didn't want to, but Pharoah and Radleigh were like 'AK? OK! Kalashnikov banter!!' which is obv meaningless, but I didn't want them going on about it the whole time if I didn't do it, plus they gave us Rambo headbands. And I was also literally a hot shot (I was in the army cadets at school) — so I drew a knob on the target in bullet holes ...

Just as we were about to go, our tour guide, a little
Cambodian guy who called himself Clive — probably gave
himself that name without realising it makes him sound like a
44-year-old accountant — called over to me: 'Yolandi! [This
was actually a pretty good stab at my name for a foreign] How
you like to fire a rocket launcher at cow? Good price. Keep
cow if you miss.'

    'I never miss.'

    'He's James Bond in a pashmina.' Radleigh said this in
a dickheadish way.

    'Jame Ban in pashmina!!! Shoo rocket!!!'
Basically, before I knew it, I had some ear muffs on and a
rocket launcher on my shoulder. I checked with Clive that I
was pointing it the right way round, as they always fire it
the wrong way round in comedy films, and we had, like, a wall
behind us, so it wouldn't have been that funny. Mostly cos
I'd be dead.

The cow was about 70 metres away, tied to a post. It looked
pretty bored, just kinda staring at me. Cows are obviously
pretty stupid because it was just chilling out on this
shooting range doing nothing, and there were bits of other
cows all round it, so it should have known. Anyway, I kinda
felt sorry for the cow and it seemed a bit pointless to kill
it cos it was just chilling. It wasn't that I was scared or
anything — I've killed loads of shit before — my dad takes me
hunting every yah — but I just didn't want to kill that cow
cos he looked like a bit of a lash hero.

    'Fucking shoot the cow *Jame Ban*, yah?' Radleigh
suddenly piped up.

    'Nah, don't feel like it.'

    'Then we'll have to keep the cow.'

    'Yah, it'll be hilah — we'll have to bring it back on
the bus, and everyone'll be like "wah did you get that cow"
and we'll be like "that's our lash cow" and we can bring it
round with us just for banter.'

    Before I'd finished the sentence, Pharoah had grabbed
the bazooka. He was a pretty good shot, hit the cow right on
the flank, but the rocket must have been armour-piercing or
something, because it punctured the cow and went straight
through, exploding at a wall 20 metres behind. The cow looked
pretty surprised, then started just writhing around groaning
so I had to use the AK to put it out of its misery, which
was a shame because I would have liked to have kept it.

Country no 17. **VIETNAM:**

You're here: Vietnam, country of a thousand faces. From the hustle and bustle of Ho Chi Minh City – still 'Saigon' to its ebullient inhabitants – to the rural splendour of the gravity-defying terrace farmers, Vietnam has it all, and its people are as welcoming of foreigners as any you'll find (as long as you come as tourists rather than conquerors!). Experience ancient culture enshrined in awe-inspiring temples, have lunch courtesy of one of the many street-food vendors, and then spend the afternoon haggling over the price of cockroaches at the unique markets before hitting the vibrant nightlife of the big city. Variety and excitement lie around every corner in the country that never sleeps (except at night!), which stands at the crossroads between East and West, North and South, North-North-East and South-South-West (on the axis of humanity and Zen Buddhism). It's a world where the colours are more vividous, where the landscapes are most emboldened, where the coastline is more dramatic; where the history is more encapsulating, where the tastes are truly more divine, where life is lived in the fast lane of the fastest motorway, on speed. There's no such thing as a holiday in Vietnam, there's only adventure. Welcome to Vietnam. Welcome to Life.

Interesting Facts:

- Border countries: Cambodia, Laos, China
- Number of motorbikes: 16 million and counting!
- Currency: The Dong Get your Dong out!!!
- Bah, bah, bah: the way to say '333', a popular beer Same as in English, but say it 3 times
- 2,709,918 Americans served in uniform in Vietnam. And they still lost …
- Mythical first ruler of Vietnam: Hung Vuong in 2879BC, founder of the dynasty of Hung kings. A lot of people call me a hung king …

Poem Inspired by Vietnahm (it's literally satirical):

Vietnahm, Vietnahm,
Suddenly it went Ka-Blahm.
The Yanks invaded,
Through innocent blood they waded,
Was this a forerunner to Afganistahn??

A lot of people say the limerick isn't the best format for hard-hitting socio-political commentary, but I'm just, like, STFU, you just can't handle the message. Then they're like, 'you can't say that to a teacher' and I'm like 'what, are you censoring me now? That is sooo Hitler. You've even got a moustache.'

Local Laws & Customs:

(Advice from the Common and Foreignwealth Office)

Illegal drugs are increasingly available in major cities. Be aware that drugs are likely to have been tampered with/spiked. Drugs are much stronger and of a higher potency in Asia than in Europe.

`I'm of a higher potency in Asia than in Europe ...`

Crimes such as sex offences or fraud can result in you being stopped from leaving Vietnam for an unlimited period without being charged, very long prison terms, or a death sentence. The Vietnamese legal system is not well developed and the standard of prisons is very poor. The Embassy/Consulate cannot get you out of prison. `But money probably can ...`

Foreign visitors to Vietnam are generally not permitted to invite Vietnamese nationals into their hotel rooms. `Same rule as for vampires ...`

Never take photographs of, or near, military installations. When entering religious or cultural sites it is a courtesy to respect local customs and dress in appropriate clothing.

NEVER TAKE PHOTOS LIKE THIS ONE ;)

It is best not to pat people on the head as the head is held to be sacred. The Vietnamese do not hold as strictly to the rule that feet should not be above the head as you will have found in Thailand. So a sex swing is back on the menu ...

Language: *Vietnam*

Chào – Hello.

Ooh, một dịp may mắn của thuốc. Điều đó không có âm thanh độchại ...
– Ooh, a lucky dip of drugs. That doesn't sound hazardous ...

Một con thằn lằn đang gặm nhấm vào khuôn mặt của bạn. – A lizard is gnawing at your face.

Bạn có muốn thử swing tình dục của tôi? – Would you like to try my sex swing?

Có điều đó không thay chố. – Yes, that does rather chafe.

Tên của bạn là gì? – What's your name?

Tôi đến từ Fulham – I'm from Fulham.

Tôi không tâm thần, chỉ có một chút của một ngày điên.
– I'm not mental, just had a bit of a crazy day.

Bạn có thể nghe thấy còi báo động? – Can you hear sirens?

Phải, không có. Tôi nghĩ rằng tôi chỉ có thể đi ngủ. – Yeah, no. I think I might just go to bed.

Orlando's Diary: Vietnahm
'Apocalash Now'

Got a bus from Phenom Penh to Ho Chi Minge City. It's funny how you take loads of buses when you're travelling but in Fulham you'd obviously just cab it. I suppose travelling opens you up to new experiences – if I hadn't taken a gap yah, I probs literally would have never used a bus. I might go on one when I get back, but London buses aren't as much fun as the ones in South-East Asiah. No one ever brings a goat on one.

***

Had a look around Ho Chi Minge, went to the Unification Palace and learnt about how the American imperialists were defeated by the 'courageous Vietcong'. Some good '60s furnishings there too. People don't have circular chairs enough. Had a big night out at Apocolash Now, a pretty cool club. That gets two thumbs up. Although we

had to move hostels because I thought I was Martin Sheen
and smashed up a load of mirrors while listening to The
Doors (I had just been crouching in the entrance). And we
were blacklisted from all the central hostels so had to
go properly far out. Our new dorm is shared with some
Israeli guys, who are OK, but also kinda mental, not
helped by the massive amounts of drugs they're ingesting.
We were all quite friendly at first:

'Oh yah, Israel, amaahzing.'
'Yes, so why are you in Vietnam?'
'We're on gap yahs. It's a British thing where you
take a year off after school.'
'Oh, yeah, well we're kinda on gap yeahs too. We just
finished a tour with the army. Got a problem with that?'
Pharoah must have looked at them funny, probably cos he's
a Muslim or something (not that it stops him being a
total lash fiend).

'No, no problem.'
'Cool, guys, so - you wanna do drug lucky dip?'
'Yah. What exactly is that?'
In retrospect, I probs shouldn't have agreed to do
something before I knew what it was. Basically they had a
bag of random drugs that they had bought from some guy,
and they wanted everyone to do a line of the stuff. I
wasn't that keen, but to be honest they were pretty
scary, and hostels are a bit like school in that you have
to do what the bigger kids say. And Saul, Walter and
David were all pretty huge.

'Whoah! I love the smell of ketamin in the
morning!' Saul was actually pretty funny, and not as
intense as Walter, the biggest guy. I laughed at Saul's
ket line until my eyes felt like popping out.

Not sure at what point things turned a bit crazy,
but whatevah was in Walter's lucky dip sent him literally
bonkers. Thinking back, it probably wasn't that funny,
but I found it hilahrious.

Walter suddenly got all wide-eyed and, like,
paranoid. Started questioning everyone about our
'intentions'. Before we knew it, he had hooded Pharoah
using a pillowcase and had marched him outside, but
everyone, including Pharoah, was just a bit too monged to
do anything about this.

After a while, me, Saul and David went to look for
them. We would have brought Radleigh along, but he was
being literally an idiot:

'We're gonna try to find Pharoah.'
'You're Pharoah.'

'Walter went nuts and took him.'

'You're in *Nuts* and took him.'

So we went downstairs and all the furniture in the lobby had been overturned. The hostel guy kept shouting at Saul about his 'friend': 'He come smash place up! You pay! He steal boat! You pay!'

Saul just ignored the guy's demands for money, and asked whah he had stolen a boat. It actually wasn't too difficult to find, because he had thrown shit everywhah on the way, so we just followed the trail of destruction to find another angry man at the end of it, shouting about a boat. He shut up once I gave him my credit card (it had maxed out anyway) and we hired one of his other boats to go after Walter who, in Saul's words, had 'gone rogue'.

We had got a boat with an engine, but it was so slow that we might as well have been on a steamship, and Walter had got a fair headstart on us so we were actually going along the river for quite a while. The funny thing was that everything is like built right up to the Mekong river edge so when you boat past you can see right into people's houses. At one point, we could even see into a club where there were strippers dressed as Playboy bunnies so we hung around for a little bit looking at them until Saul was like, 'We gotta move on. Walter ain't taking no R and R.' Further down the river we could tell that we were getting closer to Walter and Pharoah because some pissed-off villagers had come to the bankside to shout at us and throw spears — I say spears, they were more like sticks, but some of them were pretty pointy — so we had to speed up.

Shortly after that, we saw a boat abandoned at the side of the river. Walter had clearly run out of fuel and left the boat. Not far from the shore there was a crowd of villagers clustered around a shack picking something up from the ground. We went in and found Walter with Pharoah, who was still hooded with a pillowcase.

I didn't really know what to do, so I just stared at him. Saul set to calming Walter down, while David turned to me.

'The hood. You're looking at the hood. Sometimes he goes too far. He's the first to admit it.'

'Gone a bit far? A bit far gone you mean.' (I was pleased with this joke — it was pretty good given that I hadn't slept for some time.)

'You don't know what he's seen, man. Walter is

clear in the mind, but his soul is mad.'
    'What does that even mean?'
    'Not sure, but it sounds good.'
    Suddenly Walter turned his attention on me:'I
expected someone like you. Are you an assassin?'
    'No, I'm on my gap yah.'
    'You're neither. You're an errand boy, sent by
grocery clerks, to collect a bill.'
    'No, I'm on my gap yah. I have literally nothing
to do with groceries. Has he calmed down enough for us
to take the hood off Pharoah?'
    'They think I'm a god, you know? I just threw
money around out there, and now they worship me. But I'm
haunted. I saw a snail, climbing across the edge of a
razorblade ...'
    'Yeah, I think he's calm enough.' Saul was being
pretty good with him. He had probs dealt with Walter
freaking out before.
    'The horror ... the horror ...'
    'That's right big guy, the horror. Let's go home
and get some sleep.'

82

Country no 18. LAOS:

Laos, until recently closed off by its communist rulers, has now opened up to tourists like an exotic flower, ready to be fertilised by bees. Laos is quickly approaching legendary status amongst travellers for having the most chilled-out people and authentic traditional life, in contrast to the tacky consumerism to be found elsewhere in the region. Though developing quickly, it has not been seduced by the darker aspects of Westernisation and still retains charming time-honoured customs of village life such as the long-drop toilet and subsistence farming. Obviously there is a bit of a tourist trail beginning to occur in Laos, but why not head off the beaten track and make your own experience? After all, the fun of travelling here is in the travelling itself – the joy of acquaintances, the chicken on your lap during a packed bus journey, or the smiling local you impregnate at the end of the road less travelled.

Geography:

Laos is divided into three regions. Northern Laos is at the top, Central Laos in the middle and Southern Laos is at the bottom, depending on which way up you've got your map.

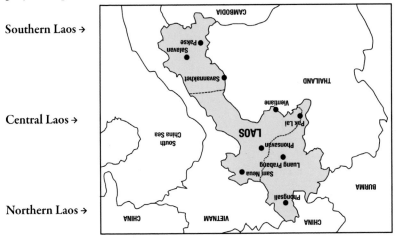

Southern Laos →

Central Laos →

Northern Laos →

History:

Laos is squeezed between vastly larger neighbours like the lacklustre filling of a service-station sandwich. It was first recorded as an entity in 1353, when warlord Fa Ngum declared himself the King of Lane Xang ('Million Elephants').

`My kingdom will be the kingdom of a million beers ...`

Fa Ngum was brought to the court of Angkor when his father was forced to flee Xiang Dong Xiang Thong (modern Luang Phabang) after he seduced one of his own father's concubines. `Lad!`

After setting up his new kingdom, Fa Ngum undermined his position by seducing the wives of his leading nobles, who decided to replace him.

`Lad gene passed onto next generation ...`

Tragedy struck at the end of the largely peaceful reign of Xainya Chakkaphat when the Vietnamese invaded and sacked Xiang Dong Xiang Thong in retaliation for the slight against their emperor who had been inadvertently posted a poo by the Lao when a hostile intermediary swapped the real package for a turd.

`The same thing happened to me with UCAS?!`

Laotian Culture:

Food and Drink

Culinary delights await you on your travels in Laos, but it's best to ignore these and focus on eating and drinking the weirdest stuff that you can.

1. Fertilised Dragon Egg – imagine chewing on a little dragon embryo. It is as disgusting as it sounds.
2. Would you like some marinated rice alcohol in dead snake and scorpion juice? Yes? Then Laos' national drink, *lao lao*, is for you!
3. Deep-fried crickets – crunchy.
4. *Laap Khom* – beef served with a sauce made from stomach bile. Bitter.
5. *Khai Luk* – fertilised duck egg – marginally less disgusting than the fertilised dragon egg, but featherier.

Language: *Laos*

Khāw thôht – Sorry.

Hàwng Nâm Yuu Sai? – Where's the toilet?

Khàwy Baw Khào Jai. Sôhk Dee Der! – I don't understand. Bye!

THEN YOU JUST SNEAK OFF AS QUICKLY AS POSSIBLE, PRETENDING THAT IT WASN'T YOU WHO DID IT.

Orlando's Diary: Laos

'Laost in Translation'

`Flew into Luang Prabang from Hanoi on an ahplane that should not have been in the ah. Looked like someone had taped the engines to the wings - spent the whole journey sitting in my seat, literally shitting myself every time the propellors stuttered. Ceiling leaked at one point.`

How can a ceiling leak on a plane?? FFS! Worst part was when the stewardess brought food around. A perfect squah of scrambled egg, dry and on its own. FML.

***

Luang Prabang is good but in the interests of major lash awahness, I should tell you that bars close at 11p.m. Apparently it's because of the communists. Literally bullshit - Karl Marx was a notorious lash hero, so he definitely wouldn't approve. Howevah, as evah, I'll provide salvation to the thirsty readah. Late-night bowling. Bowling alleys stay open and serve beer, and TBH the only way to make bowling seem interesting is to be absolutely fucked. I was like, bowling in other people's lanes, throwing Pharoah at the pins, throwing four balls at once and generally being an absolute bowl-ledge. Pure kinetic bantah. And don't ask me what I tried to polish in the ball-polisher. OK, it was my balls. Actually quite sore.

***

Tubing. Everyone's just like: 'Laos maaate? Tubing!' and that's not even hyper-bowl. It's just real. What is tubing? STFU, why don't you know what it is? OK, I'll tell you. So you get this big river, and everyone has a big rubber inner tube (from a lorry wheel) and you just float down the river from bar to bar getting more and more lashed. All the bars are themed and have crazy shit going on at them, like a zip wire or a huge swing, or a massive pile of mud to roll around in. It's like going to Thorpe Park hammered and with rides that hold the potential to genuinely maim you. So. Much. Fun. One thing to be careful of though, if you get separated from the main group, is sometimes Lao kids will spot you and hook your rubber ring in to steal your stuff. This happened to Radleigh and he wouldn't stop going on about how we had 'left him'. So watch out for this, otherwise you could have the same thing happen to you, and it gets raally boring listening to him going on.

Country no 19. BURMA:

From: David Charmon [charmond@parliament.uk]
Sent: 22 December 2011 18.12
To: Tarquin dalegend [ericbanterna@hotmail.com]
Subject: Fw: Re: Orlando in jail!!!!!!!

Dear Tarquin,

Thank you for your email and I'm sorry to hear about your infection, although it looks like you have at least avoided Orlando dragging you into his latest scrape. I had heard from a colleague at the Foreign and Commonwealth Office that a British national matching my son's description had been jailed in Burma, but I didn't think even he would be stupid enough to bring drugs across the border of a police state. You can tell him that I may be able to get him out (I was in the same house at school as a colonel in the Burmese army – not that he's too keen on people remembering that ...) and I will try to do so, but it may take some time. Though I do feel a week or two in jail may serve him right for acting in such a brainless fashion. Frankly, it might teach him something about responsibility. He only went on this bloody 'gap year' because he forgot to fill in the UCAS form, and with the tuition fee rise, that's probably going to cost me about eighteen grand, minimum. And that's on top of all the money he just fritters away. Also, when you next speak to him, remind him that his mother and I will be off skiing in Courchevel for the next week, so won't necessarily be able to receive his calls.

Happy Christmas and give my best to your parents,

David Charmon
Member of Parliament for the constituency of Brigstocke-on-Wye
Chair, Standards and Privileges Select Committee

From: Tarquin dalegend [ericbanterna@hotmail.com]
Sent: 24 December 2011 13.21
To: Orlando Charmon [thearchbishopofbanterbury@hotmail.com]
Subject: Literally in Burma

Fidel,

It was banterous to chat to you on the phone yesterday. Soz about you being in prison. I just forwarded your pa's email on to you. Hopefully you'll be out in time to have a massive new year's eve! Am also feeling less rabies-ey, so good news all round. BTW, WTF are you in prison for? Soos said she spoke to Radleigh the other day and he literally wasn't?

T-Unit

From: Orlando Charmon [thearchbishopofbanterbury@hotmail.com]
Sent: 24 December 2011 15.02
To: Tarquin dalegend [ericbanterna@hotmail.com]
Subject: Re: Literally in Burma

T-Unit,

Not much time to email. Have had to do some serious bribing to send this one.
Just wasted a lot of time by explaining that, and this computer's pretty slow. But

---

From: Tarquin dalegend [ericbanterna@hotmail.com]
Sent: 24 December 2011 15.16
To: Orlando Charmon [thearchbishopofbanterbury@hotmail.com]
Subject: Re: Re: Literally in Burma

Your email stopped midway through? Can u skype me?

From: Orlando Charmon [thearchbishopofbanterbury@hotmail.com]
Sent: 25 December 2011 07.23
To: Tarquin dalegend [ericbanterna@hotmail.com]
Subject: Re: Re: Re: Literally in Burma

Obv can't skype. I'm on a computer that takes about 10 minutes to turn on, and
had to do some serious bribing to get here, and this email is my 'Clistmas plesent'.
I'm apparently in prison for trying to bring some naughty salt with me over the
border – I always like a White Christmas!! lol. But anyway, I got caught, even
though it literally wasn't even that much. Radleigh and Pharoah were already
through customs and didn't stay to see what was going on because they didn't
want to miss their bus. It's raally spiritual, cultural and political here, but it's also
kind of brutal and demeaning? Also, 'death penalty' is being bandied about so
tell my old man to hurry the fuck up.

Merry Lashmas,

O

Inmate name: Cahrmon, Yorlanah

This inmate will be released from confinement immediately and delivered to the Office of State Security.

Authenticating officer: Colonel Yawd Mya   Date: 28/12

Personal effects:
- 3 mobile telephones
- Cash ($100)
- Degenerate scarf
- Sleeveless jacket, emblazoned from 'The University of Jack Wills Varsity Team'
- Shorts
- Bag of clothes, miscellanea incl. octopus corpse, rubber phallus, wooden spear.
- 'Flip-flops', soiled.

APPROVED

As soon as I was let out, they put me on a flight, so I didn't get to see anything of Burma. Had a few big nights in prison though; there's nothing like your own impending death for making you raally want a beer. One night we snuck in some supplies and one of the inmates, who was a midget, did some breakdancing. Chundered all over the flagstones. Best night of my life ...

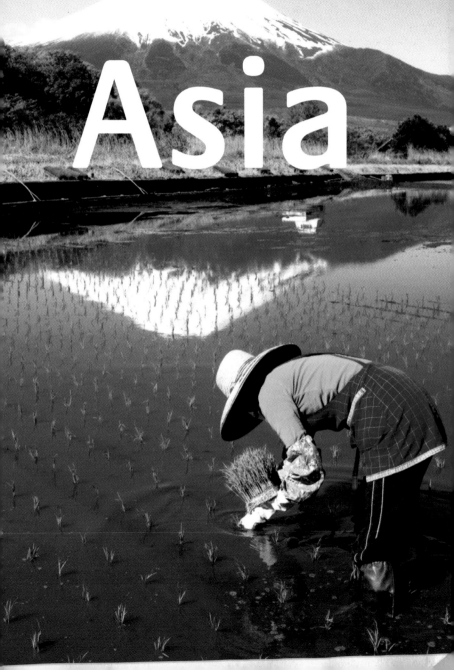

Asia

Asia

Notes:

Information and maps

I was put on a plane by the Burmese and before I knew it, I
was in Tokyah Narita ahrport. Which, BTW, is nowhah near to
Tokyah. May as well have flown Ryanah. So shit. But actually
I was pretty glad to be thah. Mostly cos it wasn't prison.

'Not Prison'

SO, little tip from the prison experience. If you get arrested
abroad, don't call your embassy or Amnesty International in case
the world media get wind of it and tell everyone you're thah.
Much better to keep it quiet and get your dad to have his school
chum release you. (Though to be fair this only raally works if
your dad's an MP and he went to school with a member of a brutal
and corrupt military junta who was 'a notorious bugger' at Eton
and doesn't want anyone to know about it.)

Larger than Europe, bigger than Oceania, greater than Africa, more sizeable than North
America, vaster than South America, more substantial than the Arctic and voluminous
than the Antarctic: Asia is the greatest landmass on Earth, but not as big as the sea, as
most of the surface of the earth is water. Yet if you were to visit this global water, you
would not find the same cultural and architectural variety as in this most eclectic of
continents. From the bustling metropolis of Tokyo to the barren Tibetan plateau, from
exotic, vibrant Mumbai to the yurt of a Mongolian herdsman, Asia certainly has much
more to offer than the sea does, even though it occupies a smaller space.

Extra Things to Bring:

1. Nothing. They make it all out
   here, and it's cheaper.

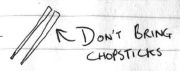

DON'T BRING
CHOPSTICKS

Japan: The big attractions

Ⓐ Find out that the largest wholesale fish and seafood market in the world smells even worse than you imagined.

Ⓑ Get your hands on the latest avant-garde Tokyo fashions in the Shibuya shopping district. NOTE— THERE'S NO JACK WILLS...

Ⓒ Visit the world's largest wooden building, the Daibutsu-den in Nara. It also holds the record for being the world's largest firetrap!

Ⓓ Visit the stunning Imperial Palace. But be careful not to walk straight through the ricepaper internal walls.

Ⓔ Learn that a geisha is not just a prostitute in the backstreets of Kyoto. They will also do a really boring dance for you.

Ⓕ Make the traditional gardens of Kyoto considerably less tranquil by kicking their raked gravel around into new shapes.

Ⓖ Accidentally eat the plastic display food in Osaka, because it looks that realistic.

Ⓗ Watch 230kg man-whales crashing into each other in the sumo ring.

Ⓘ Wander around the largest metropolis in the world – Tokyo – and climb up towers like the Sunshine Building to get the best view. You'll soon see why locals have affectionately dubbed it 'the Croydon of the East'.

Ⓙ Get inadvertantly teabagged at a traditional Onsen (communal naked hot baths) in Beppu.

Ⓚ Visit friendly Hiroshima and feel sad that we dropped a nuke on it.

Ⓛ Fukushima – don't go here (although fruit from this area can be picked up very cheaply …)

Ⓜ Use the super-fast *shinkansen* train to zip around the country, imagining how useful such technology would be back home.

Ⓝ Accidentally book a place in the stifling air-tight smoking carriage of the *shinkansen* and feel like your lungs are made of tissue when you emerge.

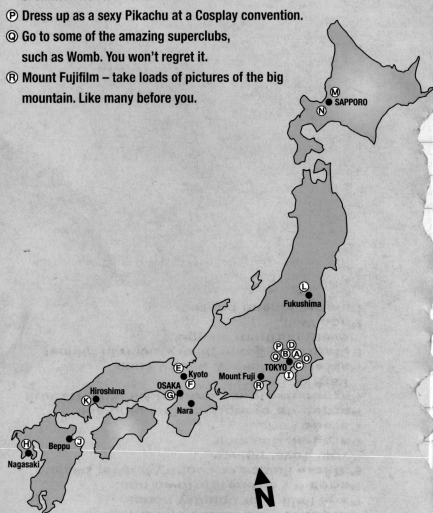

Ⓞ Visit the Yasukuni shrine and pay your respect to enshrined war criminals.

Ⓟ Dress up as a sexy Pikachu at a Cosplay convention.

Ⓠ Go to some of the amazing superclubs, such as Womb. You won't regret it.

Ⓡ Mount Fujifilm – take loads of pictures of the big mountain. Like many before you.

Japanese Culture:

FREE CAMPING?!

The National psyche

Many people find the Japanese to be initially indecipherable, and you'll probably not be staying long enough to understand them in any meaningful way, so don't bother. But in terms of interacting with these complex people, the best advice is to be polite and get them drunk. Alcohol is the great social lubricant of Japan and allows people to interact without apologising the whole time.

NOTED: GET THE JAPANESE TANKED.

The Japanese attitude towards women: while they have the same rights as men on paper, the same is not true in practice, due to a rigid patriarchal society. Women are routinely harassed on public transport (they even have a special name for it – *chikan*) by *sukebe* (perverts) with camera phones and wandering hands. Many trains run women-only carriages as a result. *GOOD PLACE TO PULL?*

Theatre

If a Japanese person invites you to the theatre, don't say Nō.

Food & Drink

Fugu:

Fugu is the Japanese word for blowfish, a delicacy served in the top Japanese restaurants. The poison of the blowfish, tetrodotoxin, is nearly 100 times more poisonous than potassium cyanide, and can bring about death within an hour and a half of consumption. There is no known antidote. It is said to be delicious though ...

Recipe for Bukkake Udon :

Ingredients:

- 4 portions udon noodles
- 4 tbsps katsuobushi (dried bonito flakes)
- For sauce: 1/2 cup soy sauce, 2 cups dashi soup stock, 3 tbsp mirin

Preparation:

Mix dashi soup stock, soy sauce, and mirin in a small pan. In a separate pan, boil udon noodles until done, then drain in a colander and cool by pouring cold water over them.

Place katsuobushi and other toppings upon the noodles and then pour the sauce on top just before serving. This liberal splashing of sauce all over the face of the noodles is what gives the bukkake noodles their distinctive name.

```
Raally tasty. Defo going to look up some more recipes when I
get back. Might just google Bukkake right now.
```

Language: *Japan*

Kampai! – Cheers!

Koko de, karaoke wa nanidesu ka? – Where is the karaoke?

Nomimono wa fukuma rete imasu ka?! – Drinks are included?!

Mōshiwake arimasenga yakuin. Watashi wa funsui ga atta to wa shiranakatta.

– Sorry officer. I didn't realise there was a fountain there.

Watashi wa ikutsu ka no bu~tsu kake ni shite kudasai hoshii.

– I'd like some bukkake noodles please.

Uwa! Subete no sutāu~ōzufigyua? – Wow! All the *Star Wars* figurines?

Orlando's Diary: Japan

'Kami-Khazi'

```
They say prison changes a man, and by
'they' I obviously mean Zorro in the 2005
epic The Legend of Zorro. And it was
certainment true of me. I realised that getting
out of jail made me much less ... bored of being
trapped in a jail. I was changéd.

***

Sooo, I was keen to enjoy myself in Tokyah, but I had
to do it on a bit of a budget because I knew if I asked
for more money soon after what my old man calls 'the
Burmah incident', he'd hit the roof. Unfortunately Tokyah
is massively expensive, so I just abandoned the budget
plan and got Mummy to transfer some funds without telling
him. In general, if people don't know about something,
they can't get pissed off about it. Just like Weapons of
Mass Destruction, or pregnancy.
```

I booked myself into a 5* hotel as I decided I was probably due some luxury after being in prison, and as Jahpan's like quite developed, there's no point in staying in a hostel to be all authentic. The room had a sseriahsly nice view and I was just having a gin and tonic from the minibar, looking out on the city of the future, when a bout of Burmese intestinal revenge hit me. You basically put up with having the shits throughout your travels in South-East Asiah, but the after-effects of Burmah were defcon level 1. Literally pebble-dashed the space-age toilet. One of the buttons on the keypad next to the loo played Chopin so that covered up some of the horrible noises, but let's just say the vibrahto on the brass section was given extra volume. After I'd finished doing battle I pressed something else and the toilet just cleaned itself with a whoosh. Amaazing. Another button then brought a robotic arse-hose into play, which literally scared the shit out of me. There was even a joystick to target where to squirt. This was all like fine, but there didn't seem to be any way of turning it off. I tried pressing a few other buttons but they just brought on more jets of water. It was like someone had decided to have a waterfight with my exposed anus. I sat there for like 20 minutes cos I knew if I stood up the toilet would juss start spraying everywah. When I did get up, actually everything just stopped, including the music. Apparently it had an inbuilt pressure sensor on the seat. This anecdote may be a bit of an anticlimax, but it's definitely for the best ...

Had a pretty chilled time in Tokyah for the first few days, but only cos I knew I was building up to a world-endingly big night out. Hit this club called Womb, and let's just say I hit the placenta pretty hard (not sure if that metaphor works ...). I was pretty drunk and a bit like hypnotised by all the lasers, but still managed to pull by juss wandering out to the smoking area and looking confused until some girls came up to talk to me. It's pretty useful that foreigns often want to work on their English. So I laid down some massive chat about how I was a political prisoner in Burmah for resisting the regime and how I had escaped (which is literally almost true) and I was well in. I left the club with Ayama, or something like that, her name definitely began with 'Ay' so I just kept making a noise like 'Ayaaaah' in lieu of her name — sometimes the language barrier works in your favour — and outside there were special bouncers to shush everyone because it was all, like, residential around. In general Japan has people doing all kinds of jobs that you wouldn't bother with in England. At the entrance to department stores you have professional bowing people to greet you and bow, then when you buy something, there's an extra person to bag it and another to smile and say 'arigato'. I wasn't wasting any effort, though, I was pursuing Ayaaaah with a

ruthless Western efficiency. She didn't want to go back to my
hotel cos it was miles away, and apparently her parents' place
was quite near (she, like almost all young Japanese people, lived
with her parents — usually people hook up in one of the many
'love hotels' in Tokyah. I thought about just going to a nearby
love hotel but actually waking up in a random house is always
much funnier — you've always got to have one eye on the anecdote
when you're travelling …). So I went back to her house and she
went apeshit at me for wearing my shoes indoors. I took my shoes
off and then bowled upstairs presuming I'd find her room, rather
than a shrine to her dead grandfather, behind the first door I
opened. What happened was the direct opposite of my expectations.
Had a little gawk then moved on to find her room across the hall.
I went inside to be faced with a mountain of stuffed toys — like
Pokemon and shit. She also had a big poster of Yoda from *Star
Wars*, which was a bit 12-yah-old boy, but I put that all down to
cultyah differences. What I wasn't quite ready for were the
noises she made during the whole sex thing. Sounded like I was
attacking her … All in all, one of the waardest sexual liahsons
of the yah so fah. Kept making eye contact with Yoda. At one
point the yelping got a bit much but she assured me that was just
something they do, a bit like getting 'L' and 'R' mixed up.

Had a terrible dream about shagging Yoda that night. 'Hmm.
Buggering me you are.' Woke up pretty freaked out and the
hundreds of glass eyes from the stuffed toys staring back at me
didn't help. Some of those things are pretty sinister looking.
Anyway, I decided to go to the loo and in my half-asleep,
totally befuddulated state, I may have taken a piss in the
dead-grandad-shrine room. I say may have. Yah I definitely did.
It was at that point I decided to
run the fuck away. Just got my
stuff and headed out the door.
There was a 24/7 convenience
store just round the
corner. Bought a
chicken skewer, a
can of cold coffee,
a beer, some fish
in seaweed and a
crème brûlée. The
guy bowed at me on
my way out and I
headed off to a
bench to watch the
sunrise and eat my
paraphernalia. Win.

From: Camilla Charmon [Camilla@Aylesburystables.com]
Sent: 10 February 2012 15:11
To: Orlando Charmon [thearchbishopofbanterbury@hotmail.com]
Subject: Japan

Hello darling,

We got a letter from UCAS saying that you'd missed the deadline today. Now I know you must be frightfully busy out there and it's great that you're seeing so much of the world, and you probably don't want to hear about boring old Britain. But applying to university is very important for your future. We've paid a great deal for your education over the years and it would be a real shame to throw that all away because you can't be bothered to fill in a little form. Your father says you may be able to get a place in clearing, so maybe you should look into that. It's possible that you feel under a lot of pressure with Daddy having gone to Cambridge, but I assure you we don't mind what university you choose. Sorry, I had to get that off my chest. I feel like such a nagging mummy! It's just been so manic at the stables lately, I feel like that Alan Sugar from that Apprentice programme. Speaking of which, one of the candidates looks just like your friend Tarquin. Your father said he spoke to Tarquin over Christmas – he seems to know more about what you're getting up to than we do! I suppose you prefer that. I would have liked a call for Christmas all the same, I haven't heard anything about what Burma was like? Sorry, turning into nagging mummy again! I hope you're well and happy and that Japan is nice. Your father sends his love.

Mummy

x

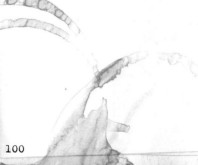

Country no 21. **CHINA:**

China. We all think we know it. Great Wall, Kung Fu, Tai Chi, Feng Shui, Hong Kong, one-child policy, Mao Tse Tung, tattoos of Chinese characters, China plates, China tea cups, China vase, human rights abuse, sweet and sour chicken. But scratch the surface of the sweet and sour chicken, and you get to so much more. In the most populous country on earth you can find more variety than in a Christmas selection box, and with even more garish packaging. So, as China takes over more and more of the world, you feel you should probably visit and see the motherland of your future overlords. Good thinking. You may be rewarded with a less humiliating servile position when the triumphant Chinese buy your homestead in Leighton Buzzard. I personally have never had any problem with the Chinese, and consider them to be the greatest nation on earth. Long may the People's Republic of China continue to prosper and the world benefit from its enlightened leadership.

Chinese Culture:

Top 5 things to see in China

1. **The Forbidden City** – Once upon a time, no one was allowed to visit the Emperor's dwelling without express permission. Hence the name. Now thousands of people wander through every year. It's not so much the 'forbidden city' as the 'forbidden if you don't pay the entrance fee' city.

2. **The Great Wall** – So enormous that it can be seen from space. This large fence was created to keep the Mongols out, due to their keenness on rape and pillage. Parts of the structure have crumbled away to be replaced in modern times by concrete blocks, giving it the appearance of a half-built Barratt home.

3. **The Terracotta Warriors** – Discovered in 1974 when a local farmer was digging a well, each soldier has unique facial features and armour appropriate to rank. Why not cover yourself in clay and join them?

4. **Giant pandas** – Watch these magnificent creatures failing to have sex and consequently going extinct. See them while you still can!

5. **Tiananmen Square** – The largest open square in the world. Camp out here and see how long it takes the authorities to move you on.

IT'S JUST LIKE SLOANE SQUAH, BUT BIGGER. DOESN'T HAVE A JOHN LEWIS THOUGH...

42. Sichuan Chicken **7.95**
Chicken in an authentic spicy sauce, with chilli and ginger.

History of China:

Chinese history is often misrepresented as very complicated, but in fact can be summarised easily in one paragraph. China was ruled by a network of kings and princes until the establishment of the Qin dynasty. When this collapsed, it was replaced by the Han dynasty, which in turn was superseded by the Wei, Shu and Wu, until the Wu were conquered by the Jin. During the reign of Emperor Min of Jin, the country was thrown into disarray by the uprising of Wu Hu. These rival territories were then reunited under the Sui, who in their decline were succeeded by the Tang. The Tang dynasty's rule lasted until it was fatally weakened by the Huang Chao rebellion, and the territory crumbled into the separate territorial units of the Zhu Wen, Li Keyong, Liu Rengong, Li Maohzen, Luo Shaowei, Wang Rong, Wang Chuzhi, Yang Xingmi, Qian Liu, Ma Yin, Wang Shenzhi, Liu Yin and Wang Jian. These went for a Song until the arrival of Kublai Khan, a Mongol who started the Yuan dynasty. Then there were the Mings, then the Qings, then a republic was founded. The Japanese invaded for a bit, and after they left there was a bit more war and some long marching until the communists won and founded the People's Republic of China. Simples.

No.37   A HALF FORTUNE

That direction is clouded so thick that east or west are not seen. Though you want to be famous in career, a chance doesn't come yet.

You should wait for a chance with patience until the time comes. Just like to hunt 2 geese with one arrow, you can get couole happiness.

*Your request will not be granted. *The patient get well but takes long. *The lost article will be found but late. *The person you wait for will come but late. *Building a new house removal are both well. *To start a trip is well, with no harm. *Marriage and employment will be well at last.

「浅草寺観音籤」の由来と心得

　お籤の習俗はそのむかし中国より伝えられ、比叡山において、日本独特の吉凶を占う百番のお籤となりました。当初は関西方面で広まりましたが、江戸時代には関東にも広がり、庶民向けに改められて今日の「浅草寺観音籤」となりました。
　観音籤には一番から百番まであり、その吉凶判断には凶・吉・末吉・半吉・小吉・末小吉・大吉の7種類があります。この中、**大吉が出たからといって**油断をしたり、また高慢な態度をとれば、**凶に転じる**こともあります。謙虚で柔和な気持で人々に接するようにしましょう。また凶が出た人も畏（おそれ）ることなく、辛抱強さをもって誠実に過ごすことで、**吉に転じます。**凶の出た人は観音様のご加護を願い、境内の指定場所にこの観音籤を結んで、ご縁つなぎをしてください。

あさくさかんのん
金龍山 浅草寺

Got raally into Confucianism while I was here. It's pretty Confucing (pun...) so I've explained it all for you. I'm literally wise.

Confucius says:

Be not ashamed of mistakes and make them crimes.

This means that you should tell everyone about all the stupid stuff you do. Even if you think it doesn't reflect too well on you or may lead to prosecution.

Men's natures are alike. It is their habits that carry them far apart.

We're basically all one great big brotherhood of man, but some of that brotherhood like to eat duck embryo, and others would just prefer a burger. Apart from that, we're, like, the same.

Have no friends not equal to yourself.

Don't hang around with banter vacuums. Or shit lads who leave you to get arrested at the Burmah bordah.

The superior man is modest in his speech, but exceeds in his actions.

If you're giving out big chat, you've got to do stuff that is more banterous than you say.

And remember, wherever you go, there you are.

I'm literally in China.

In a country well-governed, poverty is something to be ashamed of. In a country poorly governed, wealth is something to be ashamed of.

It's OK to have loads of money in Fulham, because it's got a Tory council, but you shouldn't be rich in Bangalore or Birmingham, because that's, like, immoral.

You cannot open a book without learning something.

Even this one ...

Choose a job you love, and you will never have to work a day in your life.

A gap yah is a job, right?

A journey of a thousand miles begins with a single step.

... onto an ahrplane.

Worry not that no one knows you; seek to be worth knowing.

Work on your banter.

103

Orlando's Diary: Chinah

'Chinority Report'

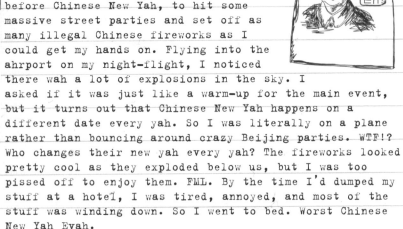

ASIA | Information and maps

I was aiming to arrive in Beijing a week
before Chinese New Yah, to hit some
massive street parties and set off as
many illegal Chinese fireworks as I
could get my hands on. Flying into the
ahrport on my night-flight, I noticed
there wah a lot of explosions in the sky. I
asked if it was just like a warm-up for the main event,
but it turns out that Chinese New Yah happens on a
different date every yah. So I was literally on a plane
rather than bouncing around crazy Beijing parties. WTF!?
Who changes their new yah every yah? The fireworks looked
pretty cool as they exploded below us, but I was too
pissed off to enjoy them. FML. By the time I'd dumped my
stuff at a hotel, I was tired, annoyed, and most of the
stuff was winding down. So I went to bed. Worst Chinese
New Yah Evah.

I can't remember what I did for the next few days. I think
I just wandered around a bit pissed off. One day I decided
to hit some sights. Forbidden City was closed. Great Wall
was average. Starbucks was shit. It was like someone was
offering me ten thousand spoons when all I needed was a
knife. Then I went to Mao's mausoleum, which was AH-maz-
ing. You definitely don't get to see enough preserved
corpses in Fulham (although you do see the wives of
Russian oligarchs, who look exactly the same after a big
botox session …).

The mausoleum was pure banter, and I bought loads of Mao
memorabilia. It was a bit annoying though when some guards
were shouting at me for trying to get a picture of myself
with Mao on my iPhone.
    '没有摄影'
    'It's OK, I just wanted to get a picture of me and
Chairman Lash.'
    '你这种行为玷污我们与伟大领袖'
    'No, it's fine. I'm a big fan - look, I've got a
Chairman T-shirt.'
    '这是不可接受的。你被逮捕了。'

Luckily at this point a random Westerner came over and
started talking Chinese at them, and they calmed down.

Then they threw me out, which was probably the best
outcome I could expect. I'd pretty much had enough of
being put in prison by repressive regimes. That activity
is just soo last yah. It'd be like, OMG that is soo yah of
the rabbit.

'What did you say to them?'

'I told them that you were here visiting the son
of one of the members of the Politburo.'

'Oh, is Gua Jin in town? I thought he had gone
travelling.'

'Erm, I don't know. I made that up? You actually
know the son of one of the Politburo?'

'Yah, went to school with him. Bit of a banter
vacuum TBH.'

'Right. Well you should probably be more careful -
these soldiers don't mess around.'

'Yah, whatevs. How come you speak Chinese?'

'I've been here for three months. Teaching in
Henan province.'

'Gap yah?'

'Gap year.'

Then we did the whole, where ah you from, what A-levels
did you take, which uni are you going to thing. He was
called Gregory, he was from somewhere called Stevenage,
which is apparently near London, he did History,
Chemistry, Maths and Further Maths, and had missed out on
a place at Cambridge so took a gap yah, and was now
going to UCL. Gregory was a classic guidebook gimp. He
always had the book in hand, and wore his rucksack on
his front to prevent pickpockets. It was pretty handy
that he could speak the Chinese though, so I let him
give me a guided tour of the city.

We went round to a few places 'off the beaten track',
which seemed to be Gregory's catchphrase. We would gawk
for a bit at whatever it was, take a few pictures and
then go to the next thing he wanted to tick off his list.
I remember at school there was an autistic kid who used
to collect bugs. He would pin them down in little boxes
and stack them up in his house. Going around Beijing with
Gregory was a bit like that. Except that unlike that
other kid, Gregory didn't have the habit of smelling your
seat after you left it - at least as far as I noticed.
After a while I got a bit bored of museums and decided we
should have a beer.

'OK, it's defo beer o'clock now.'

'I don't really drink.'
'A cheeky beer isn't drinking.'
'Cheeky or not, it's still a beer. I don't drink.'
And that was the last I saw of Gregory. He was pretty
boring anyway.

***

Gregory wouldn't have enjoyed what I did next anyway,
which was go to an illegal gambling den. Got massively
fleeced but had fun. Also great quote from one of the
gamblers who told me why Christianity wasn't big in
Chinah. 'The bible doesn't make sense for us. If Adam was
Chinese, he would have eaten the snake, not the apple.'
I was playing pool against this guy and he was just like,
'I beat you. One hand.' Then he absolutely schooled me,
holding the pool cue in one hand.
'Maaate, that's ah-maz-ing. Whah did you learn that?'
'Prison.'

Country no 22. **MONGOLIA:**

Mongolia. Would we even know it existed if Genghis Khan hadn't managed to conquer half the known world? Probably not. Yet there is more to Mongolia than just Genghis Khan (obviously, as he has been dead for centuries) even if, as you wander around this vast nation, you can't help wondering W.W.G.D. – What Would Genghis Do? Obviously this doesn't mean that you should slaughter 30 million people (estimated number that he killed during his reign) or have sex with every woman you see (DNA data suggests he was a prolific lover, with 16 million descendants alive today), but you could just ride a horse around and get some of the experience. There are a number of responsible companies that will introduce you to a nomadic family you can live with. So, ride forth, and discover Mongolia through ecotourism, it's what Genghis would've done.

GHENGIS = LAD

Mongolian Culture:

DRINK **and Drink**

Chingis Vodka: Chingis (Mongolians call Genghis this) would probably have drunk litres of this stuff if it had been around.

Airag: The national drink – Fermented mare's milk. A versatile and potent drink that not only spruces up a White Russian, but also goes well in coffee or over your morning cereal.

I basically only came here so I could do a Facebook status based around Ulaanbaanter. Not actually that much to do. Apparently it's the most spahrsely populated country in the world, so there's probs a reason for that. Lots of empty space and a few people living in yurts. It's a bit like the VIP area in Glastonbarah, but with more Mongols walking around.

Country no 23. **TIBET:**

Tibet is often termed the 'roof of the world', which obviously leads you to question why you would want to visit a roof. Surely the lounge of the world would be much more comfortable? Well, the view isn't as nice, even if being exposed to the elements makes it pretty inhospitable. Tibet is technically known as the 'Tibet autonomous region', because it faced the overwhelming power of its technologically superior nearest neighbour and got invaded and colonised. In that sense, it's the central Asian equivalent of Wales, but not as backward.

Tibet wasn't officially open for tourists until the 1980s, but now welcomes them heartily. With its bland food and limited hospitality (again, like Wales), the real attractions of this country are the scenery and its people. Visit the vast open plains of the plateau, the stunning Himalayan panoramas and the ancient religious sites, but don't talk politics.

Tibetan Culture:

Mythology

Bon and Buddhist traditions see the Tibetans as descendants of a monkey and an ogress. The monkey was sent by Bodhisattva Avalokiteshvara (who is said to have been reincarnated as the Dalai Lama) to Tibet, and one day while the monkey was meditating, an ogress disguised as a woman demanded that he marry her. The alternative, she said, would be for her to sleep with a demon and create a race of killer ogre-demons. The monkey was unsure, and returned to Avalokiteshvara to ask for advice. The bodhisattva conferred with the goddess Tara and decided to release the monkey from his vow of chastity so that he could marry the ogress, thus bringing Buddhism to Tibet. The union of monkey and goddess resulted eventually in a tribe of monkeys who became so populous that they starved, until Avalokiteshvara dug grains from the sacred Mount Meru and scattered them in the world of monkeys where they grew into crops. Gradually the monkeys evolved, lost their tails and learnt to walk upright, to talk, and to wear clothes. Their descendants are the Tibetans. *DESCENDED FROM MONKEYS? WTF?*

The Yeti

The Yeti, or 'Abominable Snowman' (so-called because of its very poor personal hygiene) is a native of Tibet, with many locals claiming to have seen it. Yetis, or 'man-bears', as they are known in Tibet, are said to be able to ride both horses and yaks. If ever chased by one, locals advise you to run downhill because their hair will fall over their eyes and the man-bear will thus be unable to see you. The man-bears also like to ape the behaviour of humans, so one way to cull the Yeti is to get drunk and have a brawl. If you then leave out some alcohol for them, the Yetis will also get drunk and kill each other.

Orlando's Diary: Tibet
'Monastery of Sound'

So, getting into Tibet has been literally a
mission. Not being funny, but it was like those
border people didn't want anyone to visit. Had to part with a
bit more of the green to get in, as they were going on about
visas and stuff. Communism's a bit waard as a system.
Essentially, no one is allowed to do anything unless you pay
loads of money to a communist.

Ran into similar problems when I arrived at the spiritual
retreat I had booked with some monks. The official kept asking
for money. Didn't feel too bad about that though, cos it'll
probably go on upkeep for the monastery and stuff. And, like, it
could do with a coat of paint at least.

TBH, I was a bit disappointed by the monks. *Tomb Raider* had led
me to believe that they spent most of their time practising
fighting techniques and generally bantering about. There was
literally no banter in this monastery. Probs in part because of
the 'vow of silence' shit they had going on. One guy, who wore
a big gold hat that looked like a Mohican haircut, kept hitting
me with a stick when I spoke. So annoying. They put me in a
room, and told me to meditate. There was literally nothing to
do. After a few hours, all my phones had run out of battery and
I'd pretty much won *Angry Birds*, so I thought I'd just do what
they said and, like, think.

Boring.

Didn't raally feel very spiritual. Thought about trying an
asphyxywank, but I didn't have any lemons so decided against.

After a while, I stopped being pissed off at being bored and
realised that in the infinite silence of my cell I could
discover more about myself than if I were surrounded by all the
distractions of my life so far. The world weaved patterns in my
mind, and I thought about humanity. I realised that these monks,
despite hardly ever speaking, interacted with each other to a
greater extent on a human level than we ever did in the West
behind our screens. Our soi-disant 'communication' technology
drives us apart rather than connecting us. I settled into the
rhythm of the monks' life – silence, hard work and communal living
– and found solace in its structure. All in all, it was a morning
well spent, and I rewarded myself with some Dico's fried chicken.

Country no 24. **NEPAL:**

Nepal, sandwiched uncomfortably between the two Asian giants of India and China like the Mawashi between the buttocks of a sumo wrestler, has long been a favourite destination for backpackers. It offers eight of the ten highest peaks in the world, varied scenery from lush tropical forest to barren mountainous terrain, and more adventure sports than you can shake an ice-axe at. Nepal has it all, and with the Maoist rebels now largely integrated into government, there's less chance that your bus will be set on fire and you'll be marched away at gunpoint and used as a pawn in their blood-soaked civil war. This is all good news for Nepal, and with more tourists flocking here every year, you can expect to see Gurkha knives adorning more and more walls, and to be regaled with tales of adventure in this exotic land. Isn't it time you said 'namaste' to Nepal?

Nepalese Culture:

Drinks

An entertaining array of drinks are bottled in Nepal and almost all of them are sold at rock-bottom prices to the thirsty tourist. `Cash-lash ratio = Win.`

Beer is conveniently called biyar in Nepali; the big three local brands are Everest, Nepal Ice and Gorka, and all are mighty refreshing after a hard day up a mountain. They are also cheaper than imported brands too.

There are a number of indigenous spirit producers such as Ye Grand Earl Whisky ('Glasgow – London – Kathmandu') which purvey rough imitations of Western drinks. These are palatable, but only if diluted into a sugary drink.

Much better to stick to a spirit that the Nepalis know how to do well – Raksi. A distilled version of the jaar or home-brewed millet beer that they make all over the country, it is served at traditional banquets from jugs poured a metre above the cup.

Holi Festival

Holi commemorates the Hindu mythological event when Prahlada outsmarted his father Hiranyakashipu by praying to Vishnu and therefore not being affected by the burning pyre he sat on, while his sister Holika – who was supposed to be non-flammable – went up in flames.

To celebrate a girl being set on fire rather than the heroic Prahlada, devout Hindus – and everyone else who fancies it – flood onto the streets with coloured powder and water bombs filled with colourful liquids. By the end of Holi, with all the swirling red water on the road, the streets look like butchers' slabs and the people like napalm victims, but it's all great fun!

Orlando's Diary: Nepal
'Erect Nepal'
● ● ● ● ● ● ●

A day after I arrived in Kathmandu,
this 'Holi' festival was kicking off.
At first, I was a bit like, 'why are
these randoms throwing shit at me?' Then I realised it
was literally religious. Apparently Hindu gods want you to
squirt each other with red liquid every yah, which kinda
ruined one of my favourite polo shirts. It was pretty fun
though, just like a foreign version of a flashmob water
fight, but instead of super soakers they have weird syringe
things full of red stuff. By the end of the day, I was head
to toe in red dye. So banterous.

***

So, some of the water from the water fight must have gone
in my mouth. And that water must have had some 'waterborne
pathogenic micro-organisms' or something, because I've been
literally shitting my guts out for the last three days.
Proper explosive.

***

It was a bit of a race against time for me and my bowels,
because I had a trek to Everest base camp booked, and it
would obv not be ideal to be still destroying the toilet when
I'm supposed to be trekking for miles and stuff. I'd pretty
much only just recovered in time to get the flight to Lukla.
Scenery was ah-maz-ing. So big — they made our mountains into
molehills (maybe ones made by giant moles). The sort of size
that makes human activity look insignificant, like dung
beetles just rolling shit around. The actual trekking was
properly tiring. Obviously trekking is just walking so
blatantly easy and you should just man up and do it without
whining, but the altitude kept making me raally tired, cos
apparently there's less aah to breathe. Also gives you a
massive headache, and, it turns out, brought about the return
of my constant companion, the shits. I tend to get a lot less
done in foreign as I seem to be shitting half the time. I
spose that's why they have less inventions and wealth and
stuff than the West — spend too much time pooing.

One night I was lying in my arctic-grade sleeping bag and I
felt all gassy. Letting out a fart when your guts are in

pieces is always a dangerous gamble, but I couldn't be
bothered to traipse out to the toilet tent, so I thought I'd
risk it. NEVER RISK IT WHEN YOU'RE LYING IN THE SLEEPING BAG
THAT YOU HAVE TO USE FOR THE NEXT TWO WEEKS. Literally a
disaster. Massive shart. Waddled out the tent into the
freezing darkness, and hit the disaster site with some wet-
wipes. The shorts were a write-off so I hid them under a
rock. Luckily the Canadian girl I was sharing a tent with
hadn't woken up so I crept back in and tried to Febreze the
scene of the crime.

In the morning, I was chatting to Tina in the tent, and she
was all like, 'How's the altitude sickness? This headache's
pretty bad, eh?' I was pretty sure I'd gotten away with it,
but it turned out that the wind had caught my hastily hidden
shit-strewn boxers and blown them onto the tent entrance
where they had frozen solid, like the least delicious ice
lolly in the world. She asked to change tent after that. I'm
pretty sure she thought I had decided to display them like
some kind of waard badge of pride. Don't raally blame her
for wanting to move TBH. There's only so much Febreze can do
for a sleeping bag in that state.

***

Everest was massive banter though. Literally.

Country no 25. **INDIA:**

Travellers have flocked to India for spices and treasures for centuries, and they still do, but now the spices are the 'spice of life' experienced in the variety of this vibrant nation, and the treasures are the gold-hearted, warm and welcoming people. And there are a lot of people! The second most populous nation on earth looks set to overtake China by 2030, rising to 1.6 billion people by 2050, raising fears in the West that they might all one day decide to jump up and down at the same time and thereby change the orbit of the Earth. But put your communal jumping fears aside and enjoy a country that has so much to offer the casual traveller. From the bazaar of Mumbai to the bizarre in Delhi to Bihar in Bihar, India delivers the action (alliterative or otherwise!). India is like its cuisine – varied, spicy, and likely to give you dysentery (or Delhi belly as it is affectionately known).

Fun Facts about India!

• India has a bill of rights for cows!

• Plastic surgery was invented in India!

• Chess was invented in India!

• The Indian government offers $25 to any man who will have a vasectomy!

'Atithi Devo Bhavah' – 'The Guest is God'

The Atithi Devo Bhavah campaign was started by the Indian tourist office as a way of enticing visitors to India. 'Our visitor numbers are down,' commented one official from the Ministry of Tourism, adding, 'but they'll soon pick up if we start deifying and worshipping every idiot who turns up at the airport. That's what other countries do, right?'

Planet Bollywood:

The Indian film industry produces more films every year than any other country: over 1,000 films annually for an audience of over 3 billion. One or two of them are quite good, too.

Indian culture: 'YOU CAN ENTER THE SAME PROZZER TWICE...'
— SOUTH KENSINGTON PROVERB

An old Indian proverb says that 'you cannot enter the same river twice', and the same is true of the vibrant, constantly changing India. The proverb is particularly apt as the story of India is entwined with its rivers. The country takes its name from the Indus river that emerges in the heights of the Tibetan plateau and flows through vastly different lowland terrain. Also emerging in the Tibetan highlands is the River Ganges, a sacred body of water that is worshipped in Hinduism as the goddess Ganga. It draws as many as 70 million people to bathe in it at religious festivals, who enjoy the sin-cleansing waters undaunted by the upriver effluent from factories and farms.

The Hinduism that draws pilgrims to the Ganges is just one of the many faiths that coexist in modern India, with members of all different religions having lived alongside each other relatively peaceably for centuries (with a few notable exceptions). India served not only as the birthplace of Hinduism but also of Jainism, Buddhism and Sikhism as well as importing Christianity, Zoroastrianism and Islam to add to the spiritual smorgasbord. Why not set up your own religion while you're here? They already worship fire and cows – why not an overweight tourist from Weston-Super-Mare? Atithi Devo Bhavah!

Orlando's Diary: Indyah

'Vombay Mix'

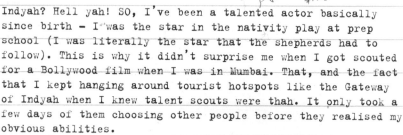

Indyah? Hell yah! SO, I've been a talented actor basically since birth — I was the star in the nativity play at prep school (I was literally the star that the shepherds had to follow). This is why it didn't surprise me when I got scouted for a Bollywood film when I was in Mumbai. That, and the fact that I kept hanging around tourist hotspots like the Gateway of Indyah when I knew talent scouts were thah. It only took a few days of them choosing other people before they realised my obvious abilities.

'Hey guy.'
'Yah, I'm defo-up-for-it.'
'What?'
'What?'
' … Hey you want to be in Bollywood film? Going to be big. Indian Tom Cruise is starring.'
'Oh, I literally cannot believe you just said that, because I'm seriously like loooving acting.'
'What?'
'Yah.'
'OK. Cool man. Come here tomorrow. 10 o'clock. 800 Rupees.'

I rocked up thah the next day half an hour late, but it was literally fine cos everyone's late in Mumbai — it's like cultural — and the bus came about an hour after I turned up. I was wearing my traditional Indyan clothes so that I'd fit in on set, and massively lucked out cos no one asked for my 800 Rupees — must have looked different to the other westerners on the bus (in general, foreigns are charged more than locals for everything in Indyah, which is probably fair enough as they're pretty paah thah, well, apart from the raaaallly rich ones). The bus bumped off down the road, then we sat in traffic for twenty minutes, and after a ten-minute drive, we were on the set of a major Bollywood film. I can't tell you the name of it - not because of the confidentiality agreement I signed, but just because it had a waard name that I can't remember.

When we got to the set, everyone was running around everywah so we just stood around aimlessly for a bit. Then I saw a food table and went and grazed thah for a bit. Everyone followed me, as I probably looked like I knew what I was doing. People always do that. We had pretty much finished off the samosas by the time someone came to chase us away.

An hour later, they decided that they wanted some Westerners as background for 'a cool party', but none of us looked Western enough cos we were all a bit dirty, and I was dressed, like, traditionally, so we had to go to the costume department and get suits to put on. They didn't raally fit very well, so we looked a bit stupid, and then we all had to dance behind the main actors, which was pretty rubbish as there was no music. After a while I got pretty bored of being human wallpaper, so I decided to find the director while we were on a break. I was just like, 'Maaate, seriously, I'm being wasted as window dressing. Not being funny, but I'm a pretty big actor in Britain.' Then I showed him a picture on my iPhone of me with Jean-Claude Van Damme (I had just run into him outside Beirut Kebab in South Ken) and another with Mischa Barton from when I met her in Boujis - James Blunt and some guy from *The Apprentice* were also in the photo but luckily I managed to put my thumb over them in time. Anyway, apparently this director hadn't seen *The OC* - WTF?? - but he did agree to give me a better part.

I got to play a villain who wanted to rape and kill the main characters or something. Apparently Westerners are generally cast as the villains because historically we are villains? The filming took ages because they kept wanting to reshoot my scenes despite me obv nailing it in one take. Was pretty relieved when we finished for the day, I'd pretty much had enough of being a movie star. It's basically just saying words over and over again. Pretty boring, TBH. They didn't even give me a sex scene, as apparently they don't have them in Bollywood films. Not sure what the point of a film is if no one gets their bits out. I suppose that's why they call it Bollywood - it's like Backwards Hollywood. Actually, then it should be called doowylloH?

BANTESH
'LORD OF THE BANTS'

From: Venetia Hourdermount [sexykittenlol@hotmail.com]
Sent: 11 April 2012 04:10
To: Orlando Charmon [thearchbishopofbanterbury@hotmail.com]
Subject: Hey Howz u?

Hiya O,

So, I know we havn't spoken since you left for the Peru, but I'm sure uv bin thinking about me. I thought about emailing u quite a few times just to hear what ur gettin up 2, but thought it best 2 wait an let u fly free like an eagle. I did hear a bit about wat u wer doin in Bankok from Soos who I think knows Tarquin. Are u still comin out to Tanzana? It's sooo gr8, really like 3rd world but also still amazing. Really glad I decided to stay here for three months as I'm literally experiencing the culture that u wouldn't if you just fly in and out of somewhere. I'm 'sema kiswahili' like a native!!! (that means talking Swahili!!!). Anyway, how long r u comin here 4? Lookin 4ward to showin u round. Must b nice to have a local guide!!

Anyway, I always thought we'd probably get back together once we'd both got travelling out of our system, espec as we wer gonna meet up in Tanzana, but I thought I should tell you I've met someone else. We shud meet up wen you get here anyway tho?

TTYL,
V x

Africa

Africa
Notes:

SHIT
ANIMAL →

Africa is a continent made up of 54 independent nations (this will probably have increased by the time you read this book), within which there are estimated to be around 3,000 tribes or ethnic groups. Africa is where humans first originated, having evolved from the great apes. It is the site of the first great human civilisation in Ancient Egypt, and was named the 'top continent to gawp at uncomprehendingly' by 7 out of 8 travellers in a recent survey by the Office for Notional Statistics.

```
Africah is probably the most spiritual continent in the world.
It's apparently whah people came from, like first – garden of
Eden and shit. It's the land of our ancestors – not saying that
the people in Africa are like less evolved, just that like the
before-people of Africa were. TBH, I don't really understand
evolution – like what's the deal with honey badgers? And what
about gay animals? And why are thah no three-legged animals?
(Well, except for me – banter!) Probs easier just to believe
that God created everything, but then, like, why did he create
the duck-billed platypus? Was he lashed? I'd probs create a
duck-billed platypus if I was lashed. Also, like, why do people
just randomly get burst appendages? I remember a kid in prep
school died from a burst appendage. Literally pointless.

Yah, sorry, Africah. SO AMAZING.
```

Extra things to bring:

1. Clothes – Even if you're going to want loads of, like,
   traditional clothes, you can often swap some of your
   rubbish old clothes for African ones. They don't even know
   which season of Jack Wills it's from, so you can offload
   your old gilet here, and get a raaally decent loincloth
   in return.

2. Food – Most African food is, like, not great. It's worth
   at least bringing some chilli sauce so you don't have to
   taste it.

3. Medication – They don't have enough of that here.

4. Louis Vuitton bags – Bono doesn't go to Africa without
   one, so these are quite on-trend.

5. Mosquito nets – Otherwise you'll get malariah. Although
   if you've got, like, eccinacceah you'll probs be fine.

6. Video camerah, iPhone iCapture Africah app – You'll want
   to put the whole continent on YouTube.

7. A perve-lens camerah – The sort of camerah that someone
   in a trench coat outside a school would have. When you're
   on safari, the animals often won't come near you, so you
   have to take pictures from far away.

8. Dollars – A lot of places don't take credit
   cards here, and there literally didn't
   seem to be any ATMs at all in
   the villages.

9. A party shirt – Major
   African figures such as
   Mugabe won't be seen in
   public unless their shirt
   is loud enough to make you
   adjust the brightness
   settings on your Mac.

10. Condoms – It's difficult
    to trust local brands such
    as 'Condomi' condoms.
    Even Africans don't like
    using them.

NOT A PIRATE

Orlando's Diary: Somaliah
'Original Pirate Material'

So, against all advice, I decided to get a boat from Indyah to Kenyah, which goes through water which is literally infested with Somalian pirates. Uh oh. Banter o'clock when I get captured by some pirates! 'Why would he get a boat from Indyah when the foreign office literally says that you'd be mental to do so?' That's what the squares would say. Then they'd be like, 'maybe he's a maverick, who just doesn't care for our rules.'

Anyway, despite the fact that I went round being such a maverick, I didn't see a single pirate, just had a raally boring boat trip, during which I chundered over the side quite a bit. I don't think boats agree with me. Or maybe it's rum. Maybe a combinahtion. At one point I thought I saw a pirate boat and got my bag packed to be captured, but actually the pirate boat turned out just to be an albatross. Scared the shit out of the sailors though.

So, when it says Somaliah above, as if I'd been thah, it's cos I literally almost went thah, and was properly in Somaliahn waters for a bit, and probably nearly got captured by pirates and was about to sell my story to the newspapers, then nothing happened and instead I just spent a lot of time playing cards with Ukrainian sailors on a ship until we reached Mombasah. At one point, I was flicking through channels on the ship's radio trying to pick up some hardcore grimy D 'n' B from the pirate radio stations and one of the sailors just went like 'You want musick, I have musick.' Turned out he raally liked Kings of Leon. 'Yeeeees. My Sex is On Fire' was exclaimed flatly several times while he danced like an injured grizzly bah. That killed an hour or two.

PIRATE

←LASH HOOK

PIRATE RADIO

I thought about going over the Kenyahn border and having a look in Somaliah, but apparently it's closed to people on their gap yahs and there's not even that much to see in Somaliah anyway. So, best advice is probably not to bother going there unless you're a pirate.

Country no 27. **KENYA:**

Take a 'safari' through Kenya from teeming urban hubs to great plains, rainforests, highlands and lush coastal strips. Kenya has everything. So much of Kenya is strange and yet familiar – you probably didn't even notice that the first sentence used a Swahili word! 'Safari' means 'long trip' in Swahili, and yet now it's as natural an English word as any other. The same goes for such words as *rafiki* meaning friend, *simba* meaning lion and *hakuna matata* which means no worries for the rest of your days. So why not take a safari, rafiki, to see the simba, in Kenya you'll have hakuna matata!

History of Kenya:

As the site of some of the earliest hominid remains, Kenya is often called the 'cradle of mankind'. One recent find has even been dated to approximately 6 million years ago, 2 million years before the arrival of Homo Erectus, the forerunner to modern humans. TARQUIN IS LITERALLY A HOMO ERECTION.

During the first millennium, Bantu-speaking farmers from West Africa moved into the region. BANTU!

In the centuries following, there ensued a competition between the Portuguese and the Arabs for influence on the coast and thereby maritime routes to the Indian ocean. These visitors brought goods, technology and of course slavery to the local inhabitants.

Ninety per cent of the coastal population were enslaved by the turn of the eighteenth century with Swahili emerging at this point as a lingua franca for communication between these various peoples. LINGUA BANTA!

PRESIDENT MWA KI-BANTER SPEAKS THE BANTU LINGUA BANTA. KENYAH IS LITERALLY THE HOME OF THE BANTS.

125

Orlando's Diary: Kenyah

'Yes We AfriCAN'

So, obviously a lot of my trip so far has been pretty, like, whimsical, but Africah is when things became raally serious. Forty-one per cent of Africans consider their living standards to be sub-saharan, and there are also isssues. My trip to Africah hopefully was able to provide a wesstern presssence for the resolvation of those isssues. I came to Mombasah on a mission, and it was a mission I had found on the internet and paid three thousand pounds for. I was working with an organisation called PovWatchAfricah and I was going to be part of the final solution to poverty.

We all met up in a hotel conference suite in Nairahbi and it was pretty exciting to meet everyone - like the first day at school. And also because a lot of people were from my school thah. I could see Pharoah and Radleigh across the room, but I wasn't in their group for any of the learning about isssues as I had sspecifically asked the organisers not to be put in a group with shit lads. Spent the morning in classes devoted to telling us about techniques and treatments for dealing with a worms infestation so we could teach this to people in villages.

A whole morning learning about de-worming. Raaaaancid.

At lunch everyone was talking about isssues and like about how colonialism was just literally raally bad except for when it stopped people from genital mutilation. Some guy had read a book that said that giving aid to Africans was actually a bad thing and the girl opposite me was like, 'why are you doing it then?' and the guy suddenly got all like, 'well, it's just an opinion ...' and didn't raally say anything else. Chump.

The afternoon was spent on something else, maybe Swahili, then we went for a few beers. The rest of the week was all pretty much the same. Pharoah tried to talk to me at one point, but I just like ignored him. TBH I'm not that bothered that they abandoned me at the Burmese border, I just find their chat a bit stale. When you're travelling, you've got to ditch the dead wood sometimes - variety is the spice of lash. The week of finding out about isssues followed by beers (lash 'n' learn) went by pretty quickly, then we were sent off to live with some random rural tribe.

The day we headed to the village was pretty exciting. We all had to get up raally early for the 4x4s that would take us out thah. I had barely been to bed when one of the guys, I think he was called Fernando, was just like, 'Orlando, we gotta gogo.' We were late but predictably the Africans were too (generally being on time only happens in the developed world).

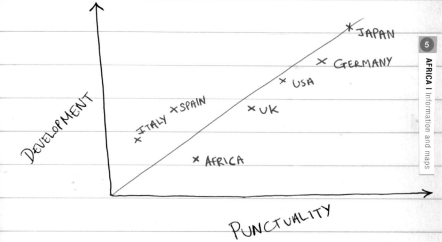

Eventually the 4x4s turned up and took us off along the worst road I'd ever seen. You know a road is bad when you see other cars and overturned trucks just left around because people can't be bothered with it any more. Being in the car was a bit like being on one of those power-plate things you get at gyms that middle-aged ladies stand on hoping to jiggle their fat up and down until it disappears (if you don't know what a power plate is, it's worth going to gym just to see the podgy women wobbling on it ...). I was so thirsty too. At one point, Herman, who was Spanish or something, offered me some water. I literally could have kissed him — in fact, we were so tightly packed into the 4x4 that it was difficult to avoid doing so at times. It was pretty annoying being trapped in that confined little 4x4, especially as Fernando kept complaining about feeling ill. After a while, I was just like, 'Fernando mate, we all feel pretty rough and hungover. Could you just man up and chill out please?'
        Felt a little bit bad about that as it turned out that Fernando actually had malariah ...

The village we were sent to (can't remember the name of it — something African) was quite nice. It turned out that we weren't actually educating them about de-worming though, we were there to build an orphanage or something. I even asked around the village to see if anyone wanted to be educated about de-worming and they didn't, so I got stuck into the building works. The work was pretty difficult, but I quite enjoyed it. We didn't get that much done as the Africans kept taking the tools from the girls and doing their jobs for them, which led to a kind of merry-go-round of work with everyone swapping just when they were starting to get the hang of it.

Over dinner, we talked about the day at the building site. Tilly was raally annoyed that we were working on a building site, and her boyfriend, Steve, was trying to calm her down.

'I mean, what the fuck do I know about building sites? Like, I'm here to get into the culture not to hammer in screws for fuck's sake.'

'Yeah, I mean they should have said that's what we'd be doing, but I think we should probably just make the best of it.'

'That's easy for you to say, you didn't have the tools taken off you every five minutes by those sexist arseholes.'

'I can imagine that was annoying, but at least whatever we're building will benefit the community.'

'Benefit the community, Steve? What do you think all those guys hanging around the site are doing? They're looking for work. Work that we're doing!'

'Well, that's kinda what volunteering is …'

'Don't be flippant.'

'I'm not. I'm just saying we should give it a few days.'

A few days later, Steve accidentally stabbed himself in the toe with a pitchfork and had to go back to Nairahbi, by which time Tilly had 'warmed to the place and really felt she had a connection with the people' so decided to stay on a bit longer.

It was actually raally worthwhile working out thah, and quite satisfying at the end when we had a big ceremony for finishing the building when the chief thanked us for 'labouring so hard in the construction of my new house. All of my people thank you for your contribution to more efficient-making government of this country.'

It actually raally meant a lot to make a contribution to the lives of these people who have nothing compared to us. Not even like food sometimes. Well, they had food. But they might not have had. But before we came, they didn't have this big house, and now they have a big house, and it was just like, hello, sense of achievement. For the whole six weeks I was out in that village, I hardly used my phone — they didn't have coverage, except on the top of a nearby hill where people would go to send texts — it was just like I couldn't be bothered, cos I was too busy helping the tribe. Everyone should have to come here, just so they realise. It's like the land speaks to you. I realised the beauty of Africa was not what we could do for it, but what it does to us. Pretty phenomenal. I wanted to stay forever and live alongside these noble people, but I had a luxury safari booked.

Country no 28. TANZANIA:

So we crossed into Tanzanah on the safari trail from Kenyah through the savannah to Masai Marah and Lake Manyarah. I had met up with the parents in Nairahbi as they basically wanted an excuse to come on safari, and I wasn't against them paying for everything, so it probably worked out well. They were a bit jumpy in Nairahbi, kept going on about how dangerous it was – 'You know the guidebooks call it *Nairobbery*.' I was just thinking STFU. My parents are literally so Western.

Safari was good banter though, got to see the 'big 5' (lion, tiger, liger, rhino, something else) which is apparently raally good as all the rhinos are dying or something. One thing about safaris though is that they're actually pretty boring for a lot of the time, cos you're just looking out the window at grass for most of it. Or worse, loads of zebras, which seem to be the African equivalent of cows. Was so excited when I first saw a zebra, but after the fortieth one, I just wanted to chuck rocks at them for being such a shit animal.

ZEBRA = RUBBISH

My old man raally liked the baboons. When a flange of baboons came past, he made us stay and watch them for like an hour. I tried to drown the parents' shit natyah chat out with my ipod.
  'Look at that male. Majestic. Did you see him bite the female? He's asserting his dominance.'
  'Nature's very violent.'
  'Camilla, you musn't think about it as violent. They live in a strict hierarchy and the male imposes order. His control over his harem benefits them all as it ensures that he mates with the best females and therefore the best genes are propagated.'

```
        My old man clearly thought he was David Attenborough.
        'I don't see why he has to bite them.'
        'He's a baboon.'
        'Typical man.'
        'Look, a rival male! I'm interested to see how this
plays out!'
        I saw from the window that the rival male was clearly
not up for a fight, so snuck off with one of the females and
did her behind a rock. The 'dominant male' was clearly a bit
pissed off with that so ran over and started attacking the
other guy despite the fact that he was mid-session, and so the
other baboon had to fight him off and then scamper away despite
having a massive lob-on the whole time. It was pretty funny.
Imagine a boxing match if one of the participants has been
given Viagra just before.
```

Introducing Tanzania:

Tanzania for visitors can often be expensive, hot and unsophisticated. But there can be few countries in the world that excite the traveller more!

In scenery alone, Tanzania is splendid to the eye. From the rapidly retreating glacier of Mount Kilimanjaro (which is said to have been given by Queen Victoria as a present to her grandson, Kaiser Wilhelm II, and therefore falls within the borders of former German East Africa) to the coral sands of Zanzibar and the petrified violence of the great rift valley. The people of Tanzania, friendly and welcoming without being servile, are as varied as the scenery from the pastoral Maasai to the cosmopolitan Chugga.

Language: *Swahili for beginners*

Mzungu – White person, from the Swahili word meaning to wander around aimlessly like a mad person. The Swahili word for a hangover comes from the same root, appropriately as most white people will wander around aimlessly with a hangover!

Jambo! – Hello! I'm an idiot tourist!

Habari gani? – How are you? (I've read more than page 1 of my guidebook).

Kiasi gani kwa ajili ya sanamu ya jogoo? – How much for the statue of a cock?

Na kiasi gani kwa ajili ya mtoto? – And how much for the child? (MADONNA ACTUALLY TAUGHT ME THAT ONE).

Hmm, hiyo ni ghali sana – Hmm, that's too expensive.

Nini bei yako bora? – What's your best price?

Utafanya naafu ya bei kama mimi kununua wote wawili? – Will you do a discount if I buy both?

OK, nami kuchukua kofia pia – OK, I'll take a hat too.

Orlando's Diary: Tanzanah
'Bantzania'

We safaried down by the Ngorongoro crater, which apparently used to be a massive volcano that exploded then collapsed in on itself. A bit like when they put loads of cream on top of your cinnamon latte in Stahbucks and the heat melts it from the inside and you get a big mush. Well, this was like a geological cinnamon latte. Saw some more animals, but I'd pretty much had enough of wildlife by then. You're not even allowed out of the jeep to pet them.

On the way back, we went to a 'traditional African village and charity programme' as part of the cultural tour. We pulled up at the village and there were some guys thah looking at us and eating a goat. The tour guide said something to them (I don't think it was even in Swahili) and they got up and started doing a traditional dance. Then we drove on for a bit more to where thah was an orphanage and we went to see the children thah. The St Mary Bethlehem orphanage was pretty grim. The kids were all dressed in rags and the room was dirty. The teacher made them sing a song to welcome us. You couldn't help but feel a common bond of humanity with the poor dispossessed children. Even my old man parted with some money for them. We drove off feeling pretty down. Didn't stop Mummy Charmon from talking the whole time though.

> 'I raally feel we've experienced poverty thah. It was quite moving. I can see why Madonna just wanted to buy them all and give them a better life. When I get back I'm definitely going to organise a tombola.'

I had sat in the back of the 4x4 and put my ipod in to get rid of her noise. As we drove up over a hill that overlooked the orphanage, I could see the children filing out. They had changed their clothes and were headed towards some modern-looking buildings that I hadn't seen earlier as they were behind some trees. I was actually kinda glad. Didn't say anything to the parents though.

Arrived in Arushah in Tanzanah with a sore arse from the lack of suspension and shit roads, but with loads of pictures of animals sniffing and eating each other and stuff. I said I'd meat up with Venetiah (Freudian slip her one?), a girl I used to see. The parents were fucking off to some beach resort in Zanzibah, which was good because I had got pretty bored of their middle-aged banter. Mummy had pretty much exhausted her anecdotes about people at the stables and the woman who she walks the dog with whose husband had an affair with a plumber. The old man just seemed a bit pissed off most of the time, but they get like that. I think they miss me when I'm not thah, and miss me not being thah when I am.

I had a day or two to kill in Arushah before I was sposed to see Venetiah, so went to the UN International Criminal Tribunal for Rwandah just for the banter. Thah was no banter thah. Just horrible genocide evidence review.

Felt pretty ill, so on the way back stopped off in a hotel for a Konyagi and tonic (it wards off malariah and gets you lashed at the same time - double win!). Went into a raally Western hotel - the sort I'd usually avoid due to having a poor cash-lash ratio, but I was still feeling a bit waard after all the war crimes, so decided to head in anyway. I was just tucking into a second K&T and laying down some serious Swahili chat to the waitress when some old randoms came up to me:

    'Orlando! We're so glad to see you. Have you come to talk some sense to her?'

    'Er, yah ...' (Had literally no idea who they wah)

    'Well, it's a relief to hear that. We've been worried sick about Venetia ever since she told us about this _African_.'

    '... Yah ...'

Obviously these randomers were Venetiah's parents. I'd only met them like four times, so it was fair enough that I had no idea who they wah.

    'Hopefully it's just a phase she's going through. I mean all her friends are in England, and how could she possibly earn money out here? And what about university? You know she's got a confirmed offer from Bristol? I mean, that's a good redbrick university. She'd be the first in her family to go to university and she wants to go _fluffing_ well living in this s-hole? It just doesn't make sense.'

    '...'

    'Sorry to go on at you. Are you meeting her here? She won't see us.'

    'No, some bar in town. I should probs head over thah actually.'

    'Give her our love. And tell her we're not angry and she can call us whenever. We have our mobiles from England.'

    'Yah.'

    I wasn't meeting Venetiah for quite a while, but her parents were raally boring me (literally didn't need to replace one set of old people whining at me with another), so I went off to find her bar. On my way out, Venetiah's dad stopped me.

'Look, erm, we're both men of the world. I have to make you an indecent proposal.'

'Er …'

'If you can break up this ridiculous wedding that my daughter is so intent on, there will be some recompense. Monetarily.'

I was just like, 'OK, bye.' I was just glad he didn't want me to go dogging with him, which is what I'd initially thought he was asking. Everything else was downhill after that, and actually some money to get my end away would be a bonus. Or a 'bone-us' if you will. Boom boom.

The place I was meeting her was properly *local*. There was like a cage on the bar to stop people from nicking booze and I was obviously subject to a mzungu tax for being too white when buying beer. Venetiah arrived twenty minutes later.

'Heeeeeeeeya stranger!'

'Heey, also stranger.'

She did literally look stranger than when she left. She had her hair all braided and was dressed a lot differently, and just generally looked a bit unwashed.

'Don't you just loooove this place? I don't really like Arusha, it's too busy and stuff. It's just, like, GOD, where are you all rushing off to? Just soo wouldn't happen in the village. But this bar is great. Much less stressio, y'know.'

'Yah?'

'But, like, it's sooo good to see you, O! It's just like, ohmygod, I haven't seen anyone from home for so long. Barely spoken English for aaaages. I was wondering if I'd forget it!'

'Yah.'

'But I'm going on. Tell me about your year – it must have been a-mazing.'

'Yah, it's been pretty banterous. I've only been in Africah for a few months, but before that--'

'Ohmygod yeah, isn't Africa just a-mazing? The guidebooks are so right. It's like the rhythm of the continent just gets into you. I feel so lucky that I'm going to stay here. Actually, that reminds me, I was going to tell you – soz for being soo mysterious on the email – I'm staying here. I've met a guy, and I know I'm a bit young, but over here it's pretty normal, and I'm getting married. Fuma is the son of the chief so he's a pretty big deal in our village. It's going to be so crazy! A proper traditional ceremony!'

I went to a few bars that night with Venetiah, but kinda lost interest when it became increasingly clear that putting one through her wasn't raally on the cards. Later that night we

were joined by Venetiah's friend Pippah who also brought along
Pharoah, as they'd both just been on safari. I'd decided I
didn't raally care about the whole Pharoah abandoning me thing
by that point — I was pretty Lash Gordon — so actually it was
good to see him, and he had also ditched Radleigh for being a
shit lad, so we decided to travel on to South Africa together.
The addition of Pippah was also welcome, as with Venetiah out of
the game, she provided a pretty welcome Strickland Banks. Me
cracking on to Pippah also massively pissed off Venetiah and
they had an argument. Venetiah called Pippah a voluntourist and
something else in Swahili and Pippah called her a slut. Me and
Pharoah did some Jägerbombs with some Germans and kept saying
'PROST!' for the rest of the evening. After her argument with
Pippah, Venetiah decided to storm off.

    'I've had enough of this *bull*. I'm leaving.'

    'Prost!'

    'Are you coming, O?'

    'Prost!'

    'Fine. Forget it. Have a nice life.'

    'Prost!'

TUSKER · FINEST QUALITY LAGER
TANZANIA BREWERIES LTD

Tusker Lager has been brewed in East
Africa since 1923. Named after the
elephant that killed one of its founder
Tusker claims that special heritage o
being the first beer in East Africa. Its
famous refreshing taste and finest qual
has earned Tusker over 16 Gold Meda
in the International Monde Selection b
awards.

TUSKER UBORA ULIOSIFIKA

CASTLE MILK STOUT

Castle Milk Stout is brewed using choice
barley grain that is slowly roasted and specially
prepared to produce a creamy, rich, dark stout.

It is the perfectly balanced combination of
the barley, pure water, and the finest hops
that allows Castle Milk Stout to deliver a
distinctively smoother drinking experience —
indeed, the perfectly balanced stout.
Enjoy the lingering pleasure.

INGREDIENTS:
BARLEY MALT, MAIZE, HOPS, LACTOSE, WATER.
BREWED BY TANZANIA BREWERIES LTD UNDER
LICENSE FROM SABMILLER FINANCE B.V.

Not for sale to persons under
18 years of age.

It's time to kick back, relax and take it easy with your friends. Time to enjoy the most a beer can offer, great taste and great refreshment - every time.

Kilimanjaro Premium Lager. Exceptionally refreshing like the people who drink it.

6 161103 659046

BREWED BY TANZANIA BREWERIES LTD.
P.O.BOX 9013 DAR ES SALAAM

PREMIUM
SERENGETI
LAGER

When friends come together the fun always begins with the first cool sip of Premium Serengeti Lager. Refreshingly crisp, Premium Serengeti Lager is the flavour of choice in making the good times last longer.

Ladha laini inayoburudisha

4 986544 233080

Jua linapozama kama wasifu wa kazi yetu fahari yetu. Japokuwa kuna mitihani mingi mbele, ushirikiano wetu umetuimarisha tayari kwa yote yajayo. Na sasa, kuna tuzo moja stahili, imekamilika, na yenye ladha iliyo kamilika. Kwa watu wenye dira, hii ni zaidi ya bia.

As the red sun sets, like a glowing tribute to our work, our pride, our tomorrows, one reward is in order. Full bodied, full flavoured, a beer for a people of purpose. Safari Lager, more than just a beer.

Safari lager, ladha kamili, sifa thabiti.

NOT FOR SALE TO PERSONS UNDER 18
STORE IN A COOL DARK PLACE

17 59
GUINNESS
FOREIGN EXTRA

Tangu enzi za Arthur Guinness huko Dublin, Ireland mwaka 1759, Guinness imekuwa ikitengenezwa kwa viungo maalum, GUINNESS sasa inapendwa na mamilioni ya watu ulimwenguni kote. Ubora wa Guinness unatokana na utumiaji wa shayiri bora, hops na kimea. Ndiyo maana watu wengi wanasema Guinness ni kinywaji bora kwao.

ZAIRE

So, I lost that guidebook that I had been using in a game of
cards with a mentalist who kept betting 'his finger' as if
anyone wanted it. Managed to pick up another one from a guy
who had loads of old books lying around though. Got it cheap
too, so double win.

Before the parents had fucked off to Zanzibah, my old man had
said I definitely shouldn't go to Zai-ah, as he had been thah
and heard it was very dodgy now, but he had had about eight
K&Ts, so could probs be ignored.

    'Democratic Republic of Congo? If it has to say it's
democratic, then it isn't! Ha.' He was massively passing that
off as his own joke, but I'm pretty sure I'd heard someone
else say that before. 'I think your mother would prefer if you
didn't go to such a dangerous place. I *know* it's dangerous.
Used to have a lot of business interests there ... or "Burundi"
as we called it – Burundi's a neighbouring country. Geography
never was your forte. Despite the fact that Burundi has no
gold, diamonds, columbo-tantalite, copper, cobalt or basic
metals, it's been exporting them since '98! Haha. But that's
just business. A lot of people would have shied away from that
sort of thing because it was too dangerous, but I made my
money by taking risks. I'm a risk-taker. Not like you lot with
your health and safety shit. It's because I'm a self-made man.
Your generation probably doesn't even know what one of those
is. OK, yeah, I went to Eton. But I was born above a grocer's
shop. I was there on a full scholarship, and those other boys
didn't let me forget where I had come from. But I learned a
lot there, about hierarchy and not backing down. It's like
those baboons. In business, you've got to have the biggest
teeth and the reddest arse. Otherwise you spend your whole
life being some else's fag. Like when MPs were being treated
like shit, having to live on rations for a bit just to
assuage the 'public anger' as if we'd single-handedly
crashed the world economy. Ha! Really that whole thing was
just about the weaker baboons snapping at our heels. It's
jealousy. We're where we are for a reason, we've got the
sharpest fucking teeth and the reddest fucking arses. And
now we get more in daily rates than we ever did from
expenses. D'you get what I'm saying? No, of course you
don't. You're fucking mollycoddled. You just think you're
born as the biggest baboon, and you deserve it, but it's all
down to my big red fucking arse and sharp teeth ...'

He then took himself to bed. Basically he was worried about me
being bitten by a baboon or something. Given that me being
imprisoned by a brutal regime in South-East Asiah had turned
out fine, I think the old man could literally just chill out
about baboon danger.

GUIDE TO ZAIRE

Welcome to most beautiful Zaire!
**Zaire welcomes you visitors from abroad as
parteners in investment and making tourists to
this most wonderful country you have seen.**

WHY HAVE YOU COME TO ZAIRE?

Zaire has many greatnesses of climate and scenery, where you will be
most welcomed by the friendly people. Maybe you have heard about our
most recent 'Rumble in the Jungle' and associating music festival with
popular young music artist James Brown? Either way, the eyes of the
world are most truly on the great Zaire. This is why such a welcoming
pamphlet was made, thanks to great generosity of the International
Monetary Fund and the World Bank, our proud parteners.

WHY IS ZAIRE MOST AUTHENTIC AFRICA?

Zaire was once occupied by Belgium which caused most heartache to the
people and unhappiness. Therefore Patrice Lumbumba along with his
great friend Mobutu Sese Seku liberated the people from tyranny and
hardship. After this, Mobutu Sese Seko became President, having liberated
Patrice Lumbumba from the office of Prime Minister by launching a
popular coup. Mobutu Sese Seko urged all people of Zaire to become more
authentic and change their names from Belgian to African form. He
authentised his name from 'Jeff' to Mobutu Sese Seko Nkuku Ngbendu
Wa Za Banga, which means 'all-powerful warrior who goes from conquest
to conquest, leaving fire in his wake'. Later, Patrice Lumbumba was
assassinated. This was not perpetrated by people ordered by Mobutu
Sese Seko, but by spies and enemies of Zaire.

WHAT ARE THE ZAIRE ACCOMMODATIONS?

Zaire has over two major hotels and some other most welcomeful
establishments all over Kinshasa, and now that foreign-owned businesses
have been taken over by the government, they are more efficient and
authentic to Zaire culture.

Are you making business in Zaire?

The answer to this question must be yes. Zaire is greatly helpful to all people who want to make business. Government can facilitate laws to help the flow of business and be most useful to foreign investment. President Mobutu Sese Seko has a great love of money coming into the country to enrich the citizen.

What are the Zaire Wildlifes?

There are many wildlifes in Zaire living in perfect forests and streams. Come to visit them all. They are too lots to list!

What is the future for Zaire?

Rich in natural resources and under the guidance of our great President, it cannot be seen that Zaire will not prosper greatly to a bright future. Peace, stability and fruitful labour will be the essence of the future decades in Zaire. For this reason Zaire is called 'The Argentina of Africa'.

President Mobutu Sese Seko Nkuku Ngbendu Wa Za Banga say:

Come to Zaire!

'There are no opponents in Zaire, because the notion of opposition has no place in our mental universe. In fact, there are no political problems in Zaire.' – President Mobutu Sese Seko Nkuku Ngbendu Wa Za Banga

See chapters five and six for Rhodesia and Transvaal.

Orlando's Diary: Zai-ah

BANTER

'King of the Swingers'

So, the guidebook must have been out
of date, cos Zai-ah is actually called the Democratic
Republic of Congah, but not *the* Congah, which is apparently
another country, or the Republic of the Congah, which is the
same country as *the* Congah, but not the Democratic Republic
of Congah. They fucking love a corporate re-brand over here.

Also, the guidebook was out of date in saying that people are
friendly here, as they're not friendly enough to open their
border with Tanzanah. Luckily my old man — despite all that
baboon-biting bullshit — was actually happy to see me going
to Congah and one of his old business contacts was able to
get us flown in and sort us out with a safari to see the
chimpanzees and shit.

Pharoah and I were picked up from Kinshasah ahrport by Louis,
a French-Canadian (everyone hyphenates nowadays) who had
worked with my old man. When we arrived, we just stood around
waiting for him, fending off people who wanted to take our
bags to the car for tips with some *non mercis*. Louis was
late-forties, slightly overweight and very sweaty. Seemed odd
that such a naturally sweaty man had chosen to live on like
the hottest continent evah, but I didn't point that out.
Didn't raally have much of an opportunity to point anything
out, as he was talking the whole time.
      'So guys, welcome to the DRC! It's pretty crazy here,
I think you'll find it's different to anywhere else you've
gone through, and you're watching it change. Man, you two
guys just turn up like that ten years ago without a clue,
you woulda been hog-tied and screwed for everything you got
within the first five minutes. Ha, shit they woulda loved
you. If there's one thing they do well, it's milk
Westerners. Hell, Mobutu used to use the IMF as his personal
bank account for decades. But who could blame him? It all
started when the Belgians colonised the place. I mean, who
the fuck puts Belgium in control of another country? It's
not even a real country itself. Who's the most famous
Belgian in the world? Fuckin Tintin. Not even real. Like his
country. Goddam Belgians.'

Then he went on for about twenty minutes about how shit
Belgium was, till we went past the university, which
apparently has a nuclear reactor, and he told us the guy

running it had smuggled out some uranium to sell to randoms,
which sounded pretty funny. He had loads of banter about
dictators and rebels and stuff, but it was pretty difficult to
follow as thah were so many of them. He also hated Italy,
Americah and the French. The only people Louis didn't seem to
hate were the Chinese.

'The compound you're staying in is up here on the right
in "Chinatown". Most of the guys I work with are Chinese.
They're pretty much emptying the place of raw materials, and
why the hell not? What're the Congolese gonna do with all this
cobalt and stuff anyway? They bring the money, the expertise,
and that canteen does a helluva noodle soup too. What these
human rights whiners don't understand is that these little
fellers are doing more to drag this country out of the hell
hole it was than those damned bleedin' heart liberals ever
did. It's just jealousy. You found out she's fuckin' someone
else and they're better in the sack. You'll be picked up for
your monkey safari by a local guide at 7 a.m., but they'll
probably be late. I'm not coming with, as I've got to see a
man about a bore hole, but have a great time.'

When we got out of the car, Pharoah was just like,
'That guy was literally a bore hole.'

***

The next day, we got picked up by a guy early in the morning.
The compound was already empty as the Chinese had all gone off
to work, so you could hear like morning animal sounds. I was
looking forward to getting back to natyah. After the drive we
got a boat, which was a-maze as it meant we could stop and
have a barbecue on a sandbank. Generally meat tastes better
when it's eaten on a sandbank.

After a few days' travelling, we finally got to see the main
thing I wanted to come to Congah for - to see the bonobo, the
'shagging monkey'. It only lives in a raally hard-to-get-to
area of the Congah, and there aren't that many of them any
more, because they've been affected by some war. A few times
we nearly saw them, but they were just swinging about in the
trees not doing anything, which was raally annoying.

Then, suddenly, we saw shitloads of them, and they'd gone from
swinging about in the trees to just swinging. The guide told
us that when groups of them get together, they bond by
swapping food and doing each other, and even have group sex.
They're also 98% similar to humans DNA-wise (would probs be
quite useful for testing shampoo etc on?).

I watched them all sitting around chilling, not really doing much except poking stuff with sticks, eating low-grade food and shagging, and it was then I realised that I had to go to uni next yah. You can't just go around watching the action the whole time, sometimes you've got to be the bonobo.

BONO

BONO-BO

Boner-Bo's!

By **Orlando Charmon** (**Gap Yah Album**) . Updated about 1 day ago

In this photo: **Tarquin Thunston** (photos), **Radleigh St John** (photos)

Like . Share

 Dicken Hares likes this.

 Cressida Fox-Smith haha, awesome! :)
February 12 at 7.52pm . **Like**

Write a comment...

COUNTRY NO 30. <u>SOUTH AFRICA</u>:

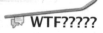 **WTF?????**   Se

| Back to Sent | Mark as Unread | Report Spam | Delete |

Between **You** and **Radleigh St John**

 Radleigh St John February 13 at 6:13pm Report
Maate, WTF is that tagged picture of the monkeys about?
Wateva Pharoah said to you, it was just for the banter.
U better not have told anyone else, cos that's just fucking
wrong. Anyway, everyone knows u just make shit up so they
won't believe u. But serious, u better not be spreadin lies
about me...

Got a bit of a waard message from Radleigh. Had literally no idea what he was chirping about, so showed it to Pharoah, and he got all like annoyed.

'God, he's such a twat. Fuck it, he's obviously given the game away. Things got out of hand in Tanzanah.'

'Banter!'

'Yah, it started out as banter. We were lashing pretty hard and we were like, we should get a prozzer. So we got a prozzer, and Radleigh was like, we should defo spit-roast her. It was just like, 2 for the price of 1. It was pretty funny at first. I was thinking, this will be literally so funny to tell everyone, then I was like, let's high-five over the top, make an Eiffel Tower! So we did that, but like, the whole thing got less funny, cos Radleigh kept making eye contact, and the second Eiffel tower kinda turned into him just like touching me. I thought at first he was playing gay chicken, just being banter gay, but I think he was actually being gay gay. I was like, no, literally not interested in that, so just left. In my culture, that sort of thing isn't allowed. If my dad thought there was anything gay being done he would literally disinherit me.'

'Yah. I thought Radleigh seemed a bit disappointed when that ladyboy turned out to be a woman.'

'So for the next few days, Radleigh was just being raally annoying. He kept saying "closet" at me every day, so I was just like, literally fuck off, I'm going to find Orlando and go travelling with him. At least he won't try to gay me up … And that's when I headed down to see you. But you literally can't tell anyone about this.'

So I'm literally not allowed to tell anyone about Radleigh and Pharoah. Writing about it is probs fine though, yah? Sounds like I was better off without those two in that Burmese prison. At least there they didn't try to make eye contact with me.

***

I bounced around Jo'burg for a bit with Pharoah but he had to go off to a family wedding, so left after a few days. We didn't raally know whah to go either, as neither of us had a guidebook (it turns out they're actually pretty useful?), but luckily I met up with Schalk pretty soon afterwards. He was just like, 'You don't need a fokkin guidebook. I'll write you one.'

SOUTH AFRICA IS THE BEST COUNTRY EVER .

- -

HERE IS A MAP OF IT >>>>>>>

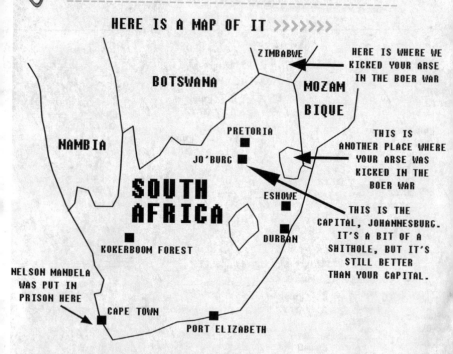

ZIMBABWE

HERE IS WHERE WE KICKED YOUR ARSE IN THE BOER WAR

BOTSWANA

MOZAM BIQUE

PRETORIA

THIS IS ANOTHER PLACE WHERE YOUR ARSE WAS KICKED IN THE BOER WAR

NAMBIA

JO'BURG

SOUTH AFRICA

ESHOWE

THIS IS THE CAPITAL, JOHANNESBURG. IT'S A BIT OF A SHITHOLE, BUT IT'S STILL BETTER THAN YOUR CAPITAL.

DURBAN

KOKERBOOM FOREST

NELSON MANDELA WAS PUT IN PRISON HERE

CAPE TOWN

PORT ELIZABETH

THESE ARE SOME THINGS WE SAY:

'BOER' LITERALLY 'FARMER' IN AFRIKAANS. BUT USED BY US TO MEAN SOMEONE WHO IS PATRIOTIC AND GENERALLY A FOKKING HERO.

'BOMPIE' A FAT GIRL THAT WILL FOKK YOU FOR A BISCUIT.

'BOSKAK' TO SHIT OUTSIDE (LIKE, 'DOES A BEAR BOSKAK?').

'DOP' ALCOHOL, TO DRINK ALCOHOL.

'GESUIP' VERY DRUNK, INTOXICATED, PLASTERED.

'LOSKIND' A REALLY SLUTTY GIRL, TITS ON SHOW.

'MA SE POES' USED IN GENERAL SWEARING. LITERALLY MEANS 'YOUR MOTHER'S VAGINA'.

'MOFSTOK' FIELD HOCKEY – LITERALLY 'GAY-STICK'. BECAUSE RUGBY IS THE ONLY SPORT.

'POMP' TO HAVE SEX.

'SOUTPIEL/SOUTIE' DEROGATORY TERM FOR YOU ENGLISH, LITERALLY MEANS 'SALTY PENIS'.

'STEEK' STAB, POKE; HAVE SEX.

'STEEKMOER' SOMEONE WHO LOOKS LIKE A WOMAN FROM THE BACK BUT A MAN FROM THE FRONT

'T.I.A.' THIS IS AFRICA. NO ONE ACTUALLY SAYS THIS, EXPECT KONTS WHO'VE SEEN 'BLOOD DIAMOND'.

THAT'S ALL YOU NEED TO KNOW.

Orlando's Diary: South Africah

'Buffalo soldiers'

Schalk picked me up in Jo'burg outside my hostel in an absolutely massive car.

'Aweh mun, get in. Jo'burg isn't the kinda place you want to be just hanging around loike a kont.'

I got in his pick-up and we drove to his house, which was like a ranch thing out in the country. On the way we went through Soweto — I wanted to stop for a picture in the bit that had my name but Schalk wouldn't let me.

Orlando West

Orlando East

Diepkloof

Mofolo South

Orlando

Klipspruit

Power Park

Armdale

Soweto

Devland

I felt touched by the poverty I could see through the tinted
windows. Schalk saw that I was obviously feeling a connection to
these people who were noble in the face of adversity.

    'Don't worry mun, it's perfectly safe to drive here. Ag,
don't believe the scaremongering they tell you abroad about this
place. No one's going to carjack us. Sith Africa has its
problems, ya, but it's a young nation, trying to build shit up
from a difficult history.'

    'Oh yah, no, I wasn't —'

    'Plus, if any of the fokkers come near the car, it's got
inbuilt flamethrowers. I fitted them myself. The whole shell is
bulletproof too.'

    We drove past 'Fochville', which I thought was pretty
funny. Schalk didn't find it as funny, probs cos he drove
past it all the time. (But then I pretty much laugh every
time the tube is going to Cockfosters.) Schalk made us get
out and look at a statue of some guy who had died fighting
the British. Apparently we had to send 4,000 soldiers to
catch him, so he sounds like a bit of a lad. Apparently he's
Charlize Theron's ancestor too, which is literally another
string to his bow.

    The drive was a bit of a mission as Schalk lived in the
middle of nowhah in some unpronounceable place past Potchefstoom
and Vijoenskroon. Afrikaans tries to fit too many vowels into all
its words.

Schalk's ranch was raally nice. It was so *real*. They even
chopped wood and shit. Schalk's dad (also called Schalk) was
exactly like Schalk, except old, and his mum was a bit of a
milf. He apparently had a sister, but she wasn't around. I was
hoping she'd take after her mother rather than craggy-faced
Schalk senior, who looked like Gordon Ramsay if he were vacuum-
packed. When I arrived, they all did something waard — they like
said a prayer thanking God for the safe arrival of their
visitor. I spose it was probably fair enough as I had flown on a
pretty budget airline.

    The next day Schalk took me bushpig hunting. Apparently
the bushpigs are best hunted at night, but we walked out in the
afternoon with our rifles to scope out a good spot. Schalk had
hunted pigs loads with his old man, but didn't usually go on his
own, and seemed a bit nervous. This wasn't helped when we nearly
walked right into a water buffalo.

    'Shut, bru — you see that?'

    'That cow thing?'

    'Mun, it's a buffalo. Fokking dangerous.'

    'It's just like a big cow. Let's shoot it. It looks
pretty random.'

'Shooting it would just puss it off. Our guns aren't powerful enough to kill it.'

'Oh, that's a shame. Looks pretty tasty. Maybe there's some pigs over thah.'

'Don't fokking move, mun. I think it's seen us.'

So Schalk made us stay still until the buffalo wandered off. Literally never seen anyone so scared of a cow before, but then T.I.A. It was dark before we moved, and I was pretty bored. I was pretty keen to head off, but Schalk had heard some pigs bantering about, so I followed him. In the end, it wasn't actually that difficult to shoot the pig, cos one of them charged at me and I just shot it. All seemed like a lot of effort to get some bacon, especially as Schalk had to finish it off with the butt of his rifle. People would probably eat a lot less meat if they had to kill it every time. There's literally something to be said for getting a few slices of stuff in a plastic packet rather than having to carry a big hairy pig for a mile back to a house and pull bits out of it. Still, Schalk seemed pleased.

We took a while to get back — pigs are pretty heavy — so the sun was rising when we returned. Schalk's sister Rosalind was just leaving the house to look after some livestock or something. She seemed impressed by my pig. Schalk wasn't impressed by Rosalind being impressed though. Once she left, he was all like, 'Don't even think about it, bru. We'll find you a nice bompie at the party tomorrow, but stay away from my sister. Rrrright?'

The next day a load of Schalk's neighbours came around for a BBQ or 'braii'. There were a lot of meats on offer and everyone was very excited. Our hog was being roasted on a spit; it was a shame Pharoah wasn't there as it would have been amusing to banter him. I still sent a picture message to him and Radleigh ...

I got the feeling that the people thah didn't raally get out much and that this was a pretty big deal as a social event. Everyone had driven over from their farms and were lashing pretty hard. It was also pretty clear that they intended to drive home afterwards. Some guy explained to me that it was fine though, because the local cop was over the other side of the room and well on his way to Lashville, Tennessee.

Schalk introduced me to some girl from a local farm called Angelica, and she talked at me for a bit, but I was largely interested in the array of cured and roasted meats on offer. TBH, I think she was too. Schalk was cracking on to her friend, so I played wingman to help him out with his 'loskind' for a bit, but I was quite glad when Schalk senior zig-zagged over to me.

'How are you enjoying the party, Orlando? It's grreat, eh? I bet you don't get that in England? You and Schalk did well with the bushpig though. People are saying it's a mean-looking beast. But don't tell Schalk that. Too much praise makes a boy weak. You know living out here is much harder than you've seen. You probably think it's all party, party, party, pig, pig, pig. But it's not.'

'Yah. I was pretty pleased when I shot it, as it was getting pretty close.'

At this point, I think Rosalind spotted her drunk dad going on about pigs and decided to save me by calling him over to look at something. Before I knew it, she had replaced him, and not only that, had brought over some boerewors and beers, which was a quicker turnaround in situation than the improvement for the British after the elimination of Boer commander Danie Theron near Fochville (I didn't mention my historical analogy to Rosalind). I was clearly well in with her, but Schalk was on a mission to cock-block me and so essentially chased her away, bringing over big boring

Angelica from earlier. Had some good lash, and sang some
Afrikaans songs, and managed to make it to bed without
Angelica getting her ample paws on my boerewors, but didn't
catch Rosalind again.

At some point in the evening, I got my lash crash on in
the outhouse whah they had made up a bed for me, and slept
happily until I was woken by someone getting into bed with me. I
was pretty sure it was going to be Angelica, so just lay back to
accept the inevitable — I lacked the strength or inclination to
fight her off in the state I was in. I realised it was actually
Rosalind — epic win! — but then fail as the outhouse door opened
again and Schalk entered.

'Hey mun, you awake?'
'Er, yah, I am.'
'Cool, you want a dop?'
'Yah, I'd literally love a bed beer.'

At this point, I felt a pinch from Rosalind under the
covers, who obviously wanted me to get rid of her brother rather
than have a beer with him, but I found the situation pretty
funny, and it probably would have been waard if I'd refused a
beer anyway. Schalk just wanted to talk at me, as usual, so I
let him, though for once he didn't want to tell me how shit the
northern hemisphere was. Instead he was all about how Schalk
senior was hassling him about not amounting to anything, and
Schalk junior resented the fact that he never took his side,
even against his rugby coach when he made everyone in the team
strip naked at gunpoint and live in the wild for three days
surviving on what they could forage and cooking eggs using their
piss. Unlike the other parents, Schalk senior thought the coach
hadn't gone far enough. Also, Schalk senior didn't think Schalk
junior was interested enough in the farm to run it properly and
wasn't even impressed by us killing the bushpig.

'I mean, that was a big bushpig mun, loike 70 kilo at
least. It coulda gored us.'

At that point, a very lashed Schalk senior entered and
mumbled loudly.

'Ag, don't embarrass yourself in front of the soutie.
That was a fucking pig, boy. I'd hate to think of what you'd do
if we still got many lions around here. My father used to make
us fight those bushpigs with our bare hands. Sorts the men from
the boys. Get me a bushpig now, I'll break its neck. We boers
have never entertained such weakness.'

'Ag, Dad, why do you have to just run everything down?'
'I'm not running anything down, I just don't think people
should go around being like swollen bullfrogs, pretending they
shot the bushpig when this fokking soft pom actually did it.'
'Ag.'

'Don't *ag* me. Taking credit for things we didn't do is not what our people do.'

'Ag, you're gesuip.'

'I'm not gesuip, and I don't appreciate a little mofstock-playing Steekmoer telling me I am.'

'I did one term of hockey, and you'll never let that go. This is your generation all over. You got this country into the fokking state that it is now! And I could bag a bushpig any day!'

At that point, I thought I should probably say something, as they were both in my room, and I kinda wanted them to fuck off so I could nail their respective daughter/sister.

'I'm literally sure no one is gesuip or a mofstock. And raally I don't think that shooting pigs is a competition.'

Schalk senior didn't like the idea that anything could not be a competition.

'Not a competition? I'm going to go out to my domain and kill a fokking pig, because that's what my people have done for generations. This guy wouldn't know a pig if it fokked him with its curly penis.'

Schalk's mother came in at this point and wanted to know what was going on, but Schalk senior just barged past and went to get his rifle. Schalk junior followed him shouting that he would also bag a pig, and that he'd do it faster. Then his mother followed shouting at both, leaving me alone in bed with his sister. Once again I win at life ...

I was just getting a cheeky nosh when all Helmand broke loose outside. Suddenly everyone seemed to be shooting (including me) and the noise was literally deafening. As soon as was practical, I whacked on my kimono and peeked my head round the door. (I was a bit reluctant at first, owing to flying bullets – I still remember what my ricochet had done to Tarquin's sister's pony.)

Outside there was havoc. Just past the ranch compound Schalk junior and senior were lying covered in blood, being simultaneously berated and treated by Schalk's mother in a stream of angry Afrikaans (I know they always sound a bit angry – but this was extra angry). Near to them was a wounded water buffalo that was just writhing around until the policeman from the party earlier came over and shot it with his pistol. The local doctor was at the party too, but was a bit too lashed to help much and was just dabbing at the blood, so someone decided it would be best to call an ambulance. As Schalk was being carted off on the stretcher, he told me what had happened between shouts.

'Ag, mun, we ran into that water buffalo again. It was fokking angry mun. I nearly boskakked. My old man tried to hit it with his rifle, but our bullets weren't the right calibre,

and he got gored by the fokker and his gun went off in his hand
and he shot me in the leg.'
    'This leg?'
    'Aaaargh! Ma se poes!! Don't poke it!'
    'Soz.'
    'Yah, but luckily the cop had a pretty big gun on him,
and he brought it down.'
    At that point Rosalind decided to try to sneak out of my
outhouse, and Schalk noticed.'You fokker! Are you steeking my
sister? You fokker!'
    He probably would have kicked the shit out of me if
he hadn't been strapped to a stretcher with a gunshot wound
to his leg.
    The next day I was driven back to Jo'burg by Rosalind
and the milf on their way to visit Schalk junior and senior in
hospital. Seemed like a much longer journey than it had been to
get thah. Probs because everyone was totally silent in the car.
Don't think I'll be invited back.

Europe

VIA
THE MIDDLE EAST

Europe
Notes:

THE MIDDLE EAST

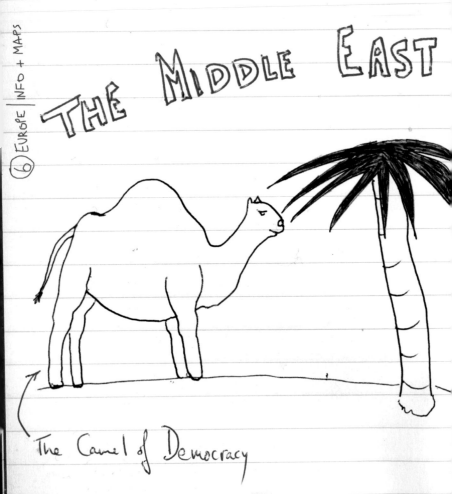

The Camel of Democracy

So, my flight home from Jo'burg got diverted via the Middle
East and I ended up with an eight-hour stopover in some dry
state – dry in that it didn't serve booze, and that there was
a desert all around. It's funny that people actually want to
live in a place that is basically desert and has no lashing
when there are so many better places to live. Probably costs a
bomb to air condition, when they could just buy a bit of
Mongolia or something – thah's loads of space thah.

    Nosing around the ahrport shops was fun, though. I
watched a load of women in burkhas buying Gucci sunglasses and
trying them on over their veils. Must have been like putting on
a four-hundred-dollar blindfold.

I was over by the giant Toblerones when I heard, 'Ohmygod, O!' from behind me. I turned around and it was Venetiah, which was surprising.

'That's surprising.' I said. 'I thought you were going to live in Tanzanah for the rest of your life?'

'Oh yah, that totes just didn't work out.'

'Why?'

'Sooo, yeeeeaaah, Fuma and I decided to go our separate ways. Literally for the best. And if I'm really going to make a difference to this crazy world, it's best that I finish my education, so I've decided to go to university.'

She kept talking to me for a while after that, but I'd kinda zoned out. I'd sorta put uni to the back of my mind, but actually, I realised I couldn't raally be bothered to do another gap yah, and should probably go to uni. After Venetiah stopped talking, I decided to call my old man.

'Hello, David Charmon speaking.'

'Alright.'

'Orlando. Where are you ringing from?'

'Middle East.'

'Good lord. That'll be costing a bomb mobile-to-mobile.'

'Nah, it's fine, cos you're paying for it.'

'Hmpph.'

'Anyway, so I've decided I want to go to uni next yah.'

'That's lucky, because you've got a place at St Andrews.'

'I thought Mummy said I'd missed the UCAS deadline?'

'You had. I called the school and told them they had to apply for you. Didn't take much persuading, as they were worried about their statistics. You're going to do theology, by the way.'

'Oh. A-maze.'

'Was there anything else?'

'Don't think so. Do you want a giant Toblerone?'

'No.'

Then the phone clicked as he hung up. And I was going to St Andrews! Not sure whah it is, but obv Kate and Wills went thah, so it must be good bants. Pretty funny way to choose a uni, but they're all basically the same anyway.

Later I ran into Venetiah's dad in the toilets of the ahrport. He seemed to think I was his best mate for some reason.

'Good news that our Venetiah chose to come back, eh?'

'Yah.'

'I know it'll obviously have more to do with her Fuma shacking up with that Canadian aid worker, but you still played your part, and I was serious about the promise I made in Arusha. I'm a man of my word. Here's something for your troubles.'

Then he gave me five hundred pounds in cash, which was a boon. Some people have more money than sense.

The Royal Borough of Kensington and Chelsea

Life Expectancy (Male): 84.4 years

Life Expectancy (Female): 89.0 years

LASH EXPECTANCY: DEFINITE

Eventually got a flight back to Heathrow. It's funny to think I went from somewhah in the middle of a searing hot desert to grey, damp Britain. Maybe that's why they make all ahrports look the same — to make the change less crazy. Though actually the only thing that really changes is the attitude of the people and their clothes. The middle-aged couple that came through arrivals next to me threw their sombreros in the bin, as if they knew Britain wouldn't be as fun. NOTE: If you want to pick up a cheeky sombrero, just go to the ahrport.

Thah wasn't anyone around to meet me except some twat flashmob singing for a mobile phone company, which was kinda worse than being met by no one. Although I did enjoy the stag do that were following them around everywah and ruining their filming by exposing themselves and shouting. Mummy had said she couldn't collect me after my arrival time had changed as she has Pilates on a Tuesday, and my old man was at work/didn't give a shit, so I headed back home on the tube. Pretty annoyed at the rentals for not picking me up though, as having a massive bag on the tube at rush hour was literally the last thing I wanted. People look at you like you're the worst person they've ever seen, as if you're taking up extra space due to being a big fattie or something.

When I got to the tube station, I decided to see if anyone was around for a pint, as the house would obviously just be a bit empty. I had put up a status on Facebook saying that I was coming back, so I checked to see if anyone had suggested meeting up. It had one 'like' and that was from my mad aunt. I decided to go over to Tarquin's house as he lived nearby and I knew he'd be up for some beers. The door to his house was ajar so I just walked in, and in the middle of his front room, there was a coffin. It could only have been Tarquin's coffin. I realised then that Tarquin must have been struck down by the rabies that he had contracted whilst travelling. I felt so sad to think that I might have done something to save my oldest friend from this horrible disease that has been all but wiped out in the developed world. I knelt by the coffin and I wept, not just for my friend, but for all the victims of this preventable disease who could have been saved.

Then I heard a voice from behind me.

'Alright Philleas Knob, what are you doing here?'

'Tarquin! You're not dead!'

'Of course I'm not. I BBM-ed you yesterday.'

'Oh yah. What happened to your rabies?'

'Didn't have rabies.'

'Why were you foaming at the mouth then?'

'Dunno raally. Dodgy drugs?'

'Yah, probs. Why have you got a coffin?'

'Oh, it's from the student protests. It literally represents the death of education. It's good isn't it? I made it from the box my new MacBook Pro came in.'

'Cool. Pint?'

'Yah.'

We then went for a pint, then another pint, and a million beers later we were stumbling down the King's Road, shouting. We were so lashed that Tarquin passed out on his own doorstep with the keys in the lock, and I ended up having a cigarette with a tramp for like twenty minutes. I told my new tramp friend (Dudley?!) about all the places I'd been and how I'd, like, experienced true poverty at first hand. If only all world leaders had encountered the truth about the deprivation faced by so much of the planet, then there would be more action.

He scoffed at me, and asked why I didn't go to Glasgow, where life expectancy in some areas thah is less than the average for Yemen or Laos. I told him I didn't go to Glasgow because it looked shit, and he agreed with me on that, but pointed out that thah was plenty of poverty to be found in Chelsea and Fulham. I said that was a good point, but that the booze was too expensive here and showed him my cash-lash map. He agreed again, and motioned towards his can of Special Brew, saying, 'It's shit isn't it. They've taxed the shit out of one of my only comforts. Governments are crooks. I hope they never legalise other drugs. Those taxing pricks would just make things unaffordable.'

It was at that point I decided to give (Dudley?!) the money I had left over from Venetiah's dad. I thought that even if he pissed some of it away on Special Brew, it was enough money to make his life a bit better for a while, and I hadn't exactly earned it. I was basically Robin Hood, taking from the annoying, and giving to the poor. I bade him goodnight and good luck and a happy St Swithin's Day (I was pissed and had decided to talk 'Medieval' like Robin Hood would). As I turned to go, I bumped into my old man coming home from work.

'Oh, Orlando, you're back.'

'Good Morrow,' I posited.

'What? Are you drunk?' he sneered.

'Veritably,' I conceded.

'But it's only six o'clock?' This surprised me somewhat, but then I had started pretty early.

'I took a little diversion via Lashford in Kent.'

'I have no idea what that means.'

My old man looked a bit taken aback by the whole situation, especially when he saw the tramp counting the wad of cash that I had clearly just given him.

'Did you just give that man a wad of cash?'

'Yah.'

'Why in God's name did you do that?'

I explained to him that he and I were different, and that I didn't view the less fortunate with innate suspicion, and that there were people out there who needed help and that my gap yah wasn't just about CV points and wanting to do it cos all my friends had, but out of a possibly naïve desire to try to improve the situation of some of the people undergoing hardships we can barely imagine. I was about to tell him that, while I could be over-exuberant, my intentions were always worthy, when suddenly a bit of Jägermeister from earlier in the day made a little reappearance at the back of my throat and I just chundered everywaaaaaaaah, all over my old man's suit and silk tie, and onto a passing Russian oligarch's wife and the small dog she was carrying in a handbag. She squealed and looked as shocked as her taut face muscles would allow, trying to jump out of the way, but she was already chunderstruck. I was so lashed I just said 'Soz,' then went into the house and left my old man to deal with the aftermath. Banterbury Tales. Best night of my life.

The next morning, I woke up in a large carved wooden canoe (who knew they'd actually deliver!?) with a half-eaten olive and sundried tomato focaccia bread. I had written a note to myself, too.

LIFE PLANS:

1. PAY FOR
   DRY-CLEANING

2. PACK FOR UNI

3. MAKE POVERTY HISTORY

4. HAVE BREAKFAST

5. CONTINUE BEING A
   LASH HERO◇

P.G.S.D
Post Gap Yah Stress Disorder

When you return from your gap yah, you'll find the Western world just so stressful. Where is everyone going? You've been used to living on *African time* and everyone's saying things have to be done *immediately* and they want the money *you owe them*. They're just soo *Western*. You've come back changed but people won't understand what happened. It's like Vietnahm, they don't know, man, they weren't thah. It's hard to readjust to civilian life when you get back. So you must do your best to educate people at length about the fact that you've got P.G.S.D. This can be done in several ways before, during and after your time away:

* By updating your Facebook status throughout:

Orlando Charmon
Orlando is sooo stressed out about packing for the trip of a lifetime!!!

about an hour ago · Like · Comment

Kenneth Le Mesurier Dick.
about an hour ago · Like · Comment

* Via the simple anecdote:

'That totes reminds me of this one time on my gap yah …'

* Through the group email:

'Hey guysssss, I'm writing to you from Basra and the scenery is just A-M-A-Z-I-N-G!!!'

* By putting pictures on Facebook:

Orlando Charmon Orlando has uploaded 82 pictures in the album 'Chat-man-du'.

about an hour ago · Like · Comment

Orlando Charmon likes this.

- By writing on people's walls:

Orlando Charmon Orlando wrote on your wall:
'I'm lashed. And in Dar Es Salaam. Put that in your pipe and suck it.'

about two hours ago · Like · Comment

- By joining Facebook groups:

Orlando Charmon likes <u>I took a gap year therefore am legally better than you</u>, <u>BANTER!</u> and <u>R.I.P the girl who committed suicide in the Westgate centre McDonalds</u>.

about two hours ago · Like · Comment

- By keeping a blog on a site like 'getjealous'. N.B. Blogging is literally shit chat.
- By bringing your iPad around with you and showing all your pictures to someone when they only met you for a cheeky drink.
- By bringing your laptop and projector around with you in case anyone wants to see all your photos projected onto their wall.
- By wearing loads of gap yah clothes when you return:

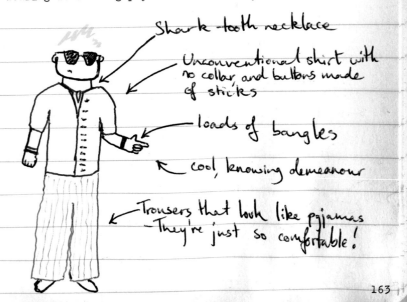

- Or you could just get a book published ...

Other shit to do:

There are also a lot of things you need to do after coming back
from your gap yah, like finding some storage space for all the
random shit you've bought, trying to read the stuff you were
already supposed to have read for uni, and getting an STI test.
Me and Pharoah decided to go for one, mostly for the bants of the
fact that the state pays someone to look at your junk. The nurse
said I was 'high risk' because of the countries I'd entered, but
later that week I got a text saying I didn't have anything.
Obviously I then texted Pharoah 'THIS IS THE NHS, UVE GOT BAD
AIDS'. He replied with 'THIS IS THE NHS, YOUR FACE IS BAD AIDS',
which was a good comeback, but the joke was on him because he
actually had chlamydyah. He reckons he got it off the prozzer
that he and Radleigh shared. Later I heard that Radleigh had
actually got it from his girlfriend, and had given it to the proz
who gave it to Pharoah. Radleigh's girlfriend, Nigella, had got
it from George who goes to Stowe, who had got it after an out-of-
control game of soggy biscuit went wrong, from the rugby captain,
Wills (they claimed it was from a foam party though), who had got
it from Celia who goes to Cheltenham Ladies College, but luckily
I had wrapped up when I was with her, unlike Tarquin.

'Travel is fatal to prejudice, bigotry, and narrow mindedness' (Mark Twain)

It can also be fatal to you if you don't get yourself checked
out at the clinic ...

CHLAMYDYAH FAMILY TREE:

ORLANDO + CELIA — WILLS

TARQUIN

GEORGE — NIGELLA — HARRY

TILLY

RADLEIGH — PROZZER — PHAROAH

Conclusion

You usually have to do a conclusion in
essays and science experiments (you've probs
made up the results of the experiment to fit the
conclusion), so I thought I'd do one. So, for
conclusation, everyone should take gap yahs, as
it's literally the best of times. Um ... I spose some things
don't raally have a conclusion. I'm about to go off to uni,
and that'll be a lot like school but with better bants, then
I'll finish that, go on another gap yah, then probably get a
job doing something banterous, not sure what. Will probs see if
one of my friends' dads has a cool job and do an intahnship
with them. The gap yah was just me stepping off the treadmill
for a bit, and at least it was a bit different. Each continent
had its own taste, flavour and smell – for good or bad – and
affected me in its own way.

Perah was the first country I visited, and it literally opened
my eyes to the whole experience, readying me to truly immerse
myself in the culture of Boliviah – which was wonderful.
Raaaally spiritual. Chile gave me the idea to import boobs-out
coffee houses, which will most likely make my fortune once I've
finished uni, so, like, thanks Chile (PS. Don't expect any of
the profits). Argentinah, Brazil, Venezuelah and Colombiah were
brief but epic – like the Sparknotes version of *Wah and Peace*
that I read so that I could justify having Tolstoy on my
bookshelf. I literally grew as a person in South Americah and
learnt a lot about love (don't leave your belongings on the
bedside table), life (an invasion doesn't count if you shout
'Banter!') and the pursuit of happiness (happiness is very
cheap on this continent, and comes much purer than you can get
in Britain).

I was sad to leave South Americah, but happy too in a way –
mostly because I don't think I would have been welcome for much
longer due to arrest warrants etc. And French Polynesia was a
wonderful place to have a drink and wait for the heat to die
down (even if Mummy didn't want me to go to a poly ...). Then
onwards and to Fiji, whah I learned that there were cannibals
on the King's Road (but I knew that already ...). I went from
the ingestion of humans in Fiji, to the egestion of a human in
New Zealand, specifically an airborne, naked one. And more
specifically, all over himself. Then it was on to the main
event of Oceania – Australiah, which was nothing like the film
Australia, in that it was actually amusing and didn't star Hugh

Jackman. I could say that Oceania was well ticked-off, but I stuck my head around the door of Papua New Guinea anyway for good measure.

South-East Asiah had a lot to live up to, and like most of its restaurants, it delivered. There were highs, such as the chemically induced highs of Indonesiah, the chemically induced highs of Malaysiah, the chemically induced highs of Thailand, the chemically induced highs of Cambodiah, the chemically induced highs of Vietnahm and the chemically induced highs of Laos, and there were lows, such as ... Erm, can't raally remember any lows. Oh, except for that one time when I was imprisoned by a brutal military dictatorship in Burmah, but even that turned out better than it might have.

Japan was literally a feast for the eyes — but then that's not surprising as I went from a prison cell to the nation that's most fond of neon lighting. Then on to China, land of lucky gold plastic cats that tap on the window. I obviously bought one and called it Chairman Miaow. But then I put aside childish things and my life became much deeper and more introspective in Tibet, and the religious experience continued into Nepal — even if the ingestion of Holy Water caused a schism in my bowels. Movie stardom turned out to be harder work than expected in Indyah (will probs just become a celeb through reality TV or something instead).

From Indyah I set out on my journey into the heart of darkness, and it was beset with difficulties. I narrowly escaped being captured by pirates and thereby becoming a hostage to my own celebrity, but survived to reach Kenyah. I did my best to save the world for a few weeks before moving on to Tanzanah, then Zai-ah, where I came to appreciate natyah and the animal kingdom. Made me wonder if there are aliens looking down on Earth right now thinking that we look as pointless as zebras — if so, maybe asteroids are just them throwing rocks at us for being rubbish animals? But it was South Africah where I saw what separates us from the beasts — love, compassion and a .22 rifle.

Scenery has changed, friends have come and gone and come again, but it has all been an experience. Foreigns might dress a little differently, act oddly and smell a bit worse, but they teach you a lot about yourself. I feel I know myself better than at the beginning of the yah. I guess I've literally found myself (cliché.com!). A gap yah promotes independent thinking, rather than just following the herd like you would at school.

I remember one time at school, we were on a coach on the way back from a rugby match, playing 'down or gay' – which is basically whah you drink the drink to prove you're a lad – and then Radleigh shouted: 'Naked or Gay!' Everyone got naked to prove they weren't a gay, and they did it without thinking. Although that was pretty banterous so I suppose it's not that good an example.

I guess it's like cats raally, some can play the piano, and others can't, but under it all, every cat has the potential to be hilahrious on the internet, and that should be realised. Raally, we've all got to be more like the piano-playing cat, and seize the YouTube. Waste no more time discussing what a hilahrious cat should be. Be One. You wouldn't want to get to eighty and realise you've got no banter. Not that I'll live that long. Being old looks boring.

Noun

appendage (*plural* appendages)

1. an external body part that projects from the body
2. a natural prolongation or projection from a part of any organism
3. a part that is joined to something larger

DRINKING GAMES!!

1. DRINK WHILE YOU THINK:
   - Someone says the name of someone famous,
     eg: Keith Chegwin.
   - The next person has to say the name of someone
     else, whose name begins with the letter of the
     previous name's surname, eg: Charlie Sheen. They
     can't repeat a name from earlier in the game.
   - As they're thinking, they have to drink.
   - Saying an alliterative name flips the
     direction of the game, eg: Steven Segal.

2. 21S:
   - Count up to 21 in a circle.
   - If someone says two numbers, that reverses the
     order of play.
   - If someone says three numbers, the next person in
     order is skipped.
   - The person who ends up saying 21 downs their
     drink and gets to make up a new rule, eg
     everyone must replace the number 5 with the
     word 'skin' or the number 8 with 'Tarquin
     loves the cock'.

3. DRINK:
   - Point at someone and say 'drink'. They have to
     drink. Then they point at someone.

4. YEE-HAH:
   - Go around in a circle saying 'Yee-hah' loudly
     at each other.
   - There are other rules, but I can't remember
     them. Those are the basics.

TOP TEN TIPS FOR WRITING A TRAVEL BLOG

1. Be amazed by everything you see, and say how it's really 'different'.

2. Make little jokes to people you know will read it (Mum – you'll like this rule!!).

3. Say how much everything costs, and compare it to how much it would cost at home. 'This book was only 12 million Zimbabwean dollars! That's like nothing – I'd barely get a Clarkson book for that at home!'

4. Make sure you refer to Africa as if it's a country. 'God, I thought Africa was supposed to be hot – can't believe it's cold lol.'

5. Don't worry about spellign and grammer. You're too busy having adventures for that.

6. Shrten evrythin, so u hav mor time 2 rite.

7. Use lots of exclamation marks!!!!!!!!!! Can't ever be too many!!!!!!!!!!

8. Be surprised when the transport infrastructure and cultural mores don't conform to your expectations. 'The train was 20 mins late, but then T.I.A. And it had about 40 people in each carriage – it's like they've never heard of Health & Safety ROFLMAO.'

9. Get overly excited when you see something familiar to you. 'OMG OMG OMG THEY'VE GOT A NANDO'S!!!!!'

10. Be sooo sad to go, but realise that you've gone on a journey as a person.

TOP CHUMPS!!!

Schalk

 South Africa

Age: 19

Banter rating: 2/10

Lash ability: 8/10

Hospitality: 10/10

Special power: Eye gouge

Pharoah

 S.Ken/Egypt

Age: 19

Banter rating: 7/10

Lash ability: 6/10

Hospitality: Not sure he's allowed back into Egypt.

Special power: Spit roast

Orlando

 Lashville

Age: 19

Banter rating: 11/10

Lash ability: 11/10

Hospitality: 11/10

Special power: Rocket launcher

174

Tarquin

 Banterbury

Age: 18

Banter rating: 0/10

Lash ability: 0/10

Hospitality: 0/10

Special power: Getting rabies

Javez

 Barcelona

Age: 32

Banter rating: 8/10

Lash ability: 9/10

Hospitality: 8/10

Special power: Special powder

Hugo Chavez

 Venezuela

Age: Raally old

Banter rating: 7/10

Lash ability: 4/10

Hospitality: 8/10

Special power: Presidenting

Juliette

Papeete

Age: 30s?

Banter rating: 5/10

Lash ability: 5/10

Hospitality: 2/10

Special power: Shemale

Hugo

Somewhere shit?

Age: 22

Banter rating: -5/10

Lash ability: 2/10

Hospitality: 2/10

Special power: Boat

Kurt

America

Age: 24

Banter rating: 1/10

Lash ability: -1/10

Hospitality: 1/10

Special power: Bungee pooing

Julie

 Shropshire

Age: 37

Banter rating: 3/10

Lash ability: 3/10

Hospitality: 9/10

Special power: Paying for stuff

Clive

 Cambodia

Age: 25

Banter rating: 7/10

Lash ability: Unknown

Hospitality: 6/10

Special power: Supplying cows

Walter

Israel

Age: 25

Banter rating: 8/10

Lash ability: 2/10

Hospitality: 0/10

Special power: Going mental

Ayaaah

 Tokyo

Age: 18 (probably???)

Banter rating: 2/10

Lash ability: 5/10

Hospitality: 10/10

Special power: Squeaking

Gregory

Stevenage

Age: 19

Banter rating: 1/10

Lash ability: N/A

Hospitality: 3/10

Special power: Reading books

Venetia

 Cheltenham

Age: 19

Banter rating: 3/10

Lash ability: 4/10

Hospitality: 5/10

Special power: Saving the world

Louis

 French-Canadia

Age: 47

Banter rating: 2/10

Lash ability: Unknown

Hygiene: 1/10

Special power: Hating Belgians

Rosalind

 South Africa

Age: 18

Banter rating: 8/10

Lash ability: 8/10

Hospitality: 10/10

Special power: Undercover

Water buffalo

 South Africa

Age: Unknown

Banter rating: 10/10

Lash ability: 10/10

Hospitality: 0/10

Special power: Goring

Emergency Contact Numbers:

Foreign and Commonwealth Office: 020 7008 1500

Daddy: 020 7219 3117

Daddy's PA: 020 7219 3000

JACK WILLS: 0845 262 5225

FINAL THOUGHTS

That's it. And if you've read this far, that means you're now
well prepared to go on a gap yah and become a lash hero. So go
forth and prosper. Let a thousand flowers bloom. Bring your
gilets and UGGs to every corner of the world, and if you should
vom, think only this: that there's some corner of a foreign land
that is forever Fulham.

GAP YAH STATISTICS:

- TOTAL EXPENDITURE: UNKNOWN
- ALCOHOLIC UNITS CONSUMED: UNVERIFIABLE
- BANTER: UNQUANTIFIABLE

ORLANDO NEEDS **YOU** TO TAKE A GAP YAH

Notes:

JUST TRYING
OUT A NEW PEN

Orlando

Orlando

Orlando.

Orlando

Orlando ☆

Orlando ☆

Orlando

☆RLANDO

Orlando

JUST PRACTISING
SIGNATURE

HAD TO PRETEND
TO WRITE ON MY
BOLLYWOOD FILM

chalk

DID THIS WHEN I
WAS OFF MY PEANUT
—NOT SURE WHAT IT
MEANS?

THE RITZ LONDON

MORE BOOZE PLEASE

—JUST PUT IT ON THE TAB FOR ROOM 301
I'M PRETTY SURE THEY WON'T MIND

150 Piccadilly, London W1J 9BR
Enquire@theritzlondon.com

Telephone: +44 (0)20 7493 8181
Facsimile: +44 (0)20 7493 2687